Blessed Contradictions

Blessed Contradictions

How the Bible Contradicts and Completes Itself

Michael Anderson

WIPF & STOCK · Eugene, Oregon

BLESSED CONTRADICTIONS
How the Bible contradicts and completes itself

Wipf & Stock
An Imprint of Wipf and Stock Publishers
199 W. 8th Ave., Suite 3
Eugene, OR 97401

www.wipfandstock.com

PAPERBACK ISBN: 978-1-7252-5802-0
HARDCOVER ISBN: 978-1-7252-5803-7
EBOOK ISBN: 978-1-7252-5804-4

Manufactured in the U.S.A.   01/29/20

This book is dedicated to my wife, Patty, daughter, Sara, and the members and friends of Holy Spirit Lutheran Church.

Contents

Preface

THIS BOOK IS AN effort to record some of the insights discovered and shared with students during three decades of biblical study. For thirty years I have used the Crossways Bible Study guide, a two-year program developed by the Reverend Harry Wendt, to teach an introduction to the Bible with members and friends of Holy Spirit Lutheran Church in Kirkland, Washington. I am indebted to Pastor Wendt and his program for introducing me to a form of Bible study which considers the breadth of biblical history—how Scripture is to be read as a grand, integrated story where one part of the Bible relates to other parts. In contrast to this broad overview approach to the Bible, my education typically focused on specific biblical books and individual verses. Teaching the entire Bible in two years with one class period per week forced teacher and students to consider the biblical narrative in overview.

Some amazing discoveries result from using an overview as a method of study, none more important than the realization that the writers of the Bible often contradict each other. One biblical writer/theologian will emphasize a point of theology while another writer will focus on something quite the opposite. Typically, when we study and teach the Bible we try to minimize differences between biblical writers but why not let the contradictions stand? In fact, why not highlight the differences between books and writers and allow the contradictions to remain unresolved? Like the facets of a beautiful gem, we view the nature of God from different angles as we read various theologians in the Bible sharing their own perspectives.

This book will be a summary of a few of the contradictions we have noticed over the years. Each chapter will highlight two biblical writer-theologians, each of whom write with their own viewpoint regarding the nature of God and humanity. Taken individually one theologian's insight will not be complete until balanced with the insight of the second theologian. Initially the two theologians appear at odds with each other, but as we think about what they have written we realize that both make a legitimate point and taken together give us a deeper appreciation for God and God's relationship with the creation.

Part One

Blessed Contradictions: Old Testament

—— *Chapter One* ——

The Creation Stories

TYPICALLY, MORE THAN ONE hundred people will gather in our church in early September to begin the two-year Bible study program called Crossways.[1] We get organized by passing out materials, discussing various Bible translations, and looking at the schedule of the classes for the coming nine months. We will meet every Wednesday evening for about an hour and a half, September to May, covering the sixty lessons. At the end of two years, we will have read the entire Bible, from Genesis to Revelation. The first organizational meeting is always filled with excitement, anticipation, and the chance to meet new friends as we begin a significant journey together.

In the second session, when we open our Bibles to the first three chapters of Genesis, the tone of the entire program is set because it is during our discussion of the creation stories in Genesis that we must consider our attitudes toward the Bible itself. Is the Bible to be considered literal? Were there people named Adam and an Eve who actually walked in a garden? Did a snake really talk? And, if we see

---

1. "Crossways" is a program written by the Reverend Dr. Harry Wendt. It is under copyright and is available for purchase from Crossways International, Minneapolis, MN.

many of the Bible stories as metaphor, which are fact, which are not? Always, in the first session on Genesis, we end up discussing the contemporary debate between creationism or intelligent design and the theory of evolution. "Which is 'true'?" people ask. "Where do you stand, Pastor?" "If the creation stories are not 'true' what else is not 'true' in Scripture?" Such questions give us opportunity to consider a very important idea related to the interpretation of the Bible, that is, how we define "truth."

Beginning in the seventeenth century with the development of Enlightenment thinking and the scientific method, "truth" has been equated with fact. What is "true" can be proven as factual using the tools of scientific research and evaluation. Truth then is merely fact. Even people who defend the creationism / intelligent design understanding of creation use the scientific framework for the definition of truth. They argue with evolutionists using the same criterion for truth as the scientific method—facts only.

As we begin Crossways one of our most important conversations is the emphasis that truth can be more than mere fact. There is truth which is beyond that which can be scientifically proven. How does one "prove" love? Or beauty? Or compassion? The Bible is not primarily a book of facts, although there are many historically accurate facts in the Bible. The Bible, as it tells the creation stories initially around the campfire, is not as concerned with how the world was created—the scientific emphasis—but rather who created the world and why. The Bible is about the presence of the divine behind the creation. It is about the mystery and the reality of evil and what God does about evil.

Sometimes I will ask my class some stories they all know and ask them the purpose of a story. For example, did

George Washington really chop down the cherry tree and then make his confession? It is a story, I tell them, which has no historical accuracy, at least using the criterion of science; but it is a story which speaks to a deeper meaning than fact. It is a story about character and the kind of personal qualities that animated our first president and inspire us. Is the story true? Yes, at the level of what is most important and vital to our nation. It is then that students share their own understanding of stories that may not be literally true but, nonetheless, are fundamentally true—Abraham Lincoln walking miles to return a few pennies in change, "Horatio Alger" stories of self-reliance and perseverance, and many of our movies, books, and art which today speak to the soul and not just of the literal facts. As we return to the Bible and the creation stories, we now can approach them with an even greater reverence than simply the scientific critique of the historian. These are stories meant to carry the deepest yearnings of the soul. They touch us with ideas of the divine, the nature of the universe, evil, and redemption.

At this point in my opening lecture on Genesis, I often surprise the class with a comment no one expects. I mention that it is just fine with me if they choose to understand the creation stories as literally fact. I also say it is fine if you understand the creation stories as metaphorically true. "In this class," I say, "You can be a creationist [and I hold out one hand to my right] or you can choose to be an evolutionist [and I hold out my other hand to my left]. In this class we will look at what the Bible teaches at a more profound level than simply scientific fact. We don't have to argue about creationism versus evolution [and then I bang my fists together]. No, we rise above the debate about science, to a third level of interpretation which views the creation stories as theology

[and I move my hands together above my head]." Conclud-
ing, I tell them that a literal interpreter or a metaphorical
interpreter must rise above their concern for scientific truth
to a higher level of theological truth.

Two Creation Stories

So, what do the creation stories teach us about the nature
of God and our relationship to God? Notice that I have
made references to the "creation stories" in Genesis. There
are, indeed, two creation stories in the first three chapters of
Genesis, each written by an author who offers a certain angle
or perspective regarding the nature of God and creation. The
two perspectives are quite different from each other—what I
would call "blessed contradictions." The first creation story
describes God as distant, remote, "other" than creation. The
theological word to describe such an understanding of God's
nature is "transcendent." God transcends this world and is
unknowable and, yet, awe-inspiring. A second creation story
describes God as "immanent"; that is, very close to us, as
close as our breath, or our heartbeat.

The first of the creation stories begins at Genesis 1:1 and
proceeds to chapter 2, verse 4a (the first half of that verse).
As my Crossways students read this first creation story, they
are struck by how orderly the story is; there is a poetic, even
liturgical, day-by-day progression to the language. "On the
first day . . . and God saw that it was good." Each day brings
into being some new aspect of creation and always the day
ends with the reflection that "God saw that it was good."

Scholars believe that this orderly account of creation
was presented by the priestly class of ancient Israel and is,
therefore, given the designation of the "P" writer(s). The

priests write their orderly account with liturgical precision and a great emphasis is placed on God's power, distance, and authority. It is quite understandable that the priests would present God with such a transcendent emphasis, after all, it was the priestly class which was responsible for mediating between God and humanity. The rituals, sacrifices, and worship services organized by the priests all emphasized God as "other" and approachable only through the efforts of the specialized priestly class.

To this day we appreciate and recognize the transcendent nature of God. Priests in many denominations continue to act as mediators between creation and the transcendent creator. Even church architecture, often designed by the priests, can emphasize the transcendence of God. As a child, I attended a small Lutheran church built in the traditional "basilica" style of ancient Rome—a rectangular shaped building with a long center aisle, pews on either side, and an altar far to the front, up a few steps and protected by a fence. Even at nine years of age, I knew that I should not go beyond that "fence" into the altar area; it was sacred and only for the priest/pastor. The greatest cathedrals of Europe are all built with a similar emphasis on the transcendent, powerful, sacred, and mysterious nature of God. It is an emphasis that accurately reflects a part of our understanding of God, but it is not the only perspective. The "P" writer has presented God as transcendent but Genesis provides a counterbalance.

The second creation story in Genesis begins at chapter 2:4b and continues to the end of chapter 3; it presents us with a much different perspective of God and creation. Its description of God is almost opposite that of the priestly writers, and yet is completely understandable and meaningful to the reader. This "blessed contradiction" actually helps us understand that, yes, God is distant from us, but God is also close to us, intimate, personal, and, using the theological word, "immanent." The writer of this second creation story has been labeled by scholars as the "J" writer because this author always refers to God as "Jahweh." Jahweh is the Hebrew verb "to be," so using it as God's name basically says God "is." It is not just that God exists somewhere, God is present, here, and will always be here. God as Jahweh, was, is, and will be. Jahweh is immanent like the air surrounding us and giving us moment-by-moment breath and life.

The "J" writer presents an understanding of God's nature which is nearly the direct antithesis of the "P" writer and so the "J" writer uses a completely different approach or method to tell his creation story. Where the "P" writers use a liturgical, repetitious style of writing, the "J" writer just tells a story, as if we are all sitting around a campfire rather than standing in some ornate cathedral or temple. The story we hear from "J" is familiar to nearly all people on earth. Jahweh creates a garden, in Hebrew, a "paradise," where Adam is created on the first day. (This is different from the "P" writer, where humanity—male and female—was created on the sixth day.) The "J" writer describes Jahweh walking in the garden, fashioning the human form from the mud of the earth, and breathing the spirit of life into Adam. It is an intimate portrayal of God, much different from the distant, awesome God of the "P" writer. As the story unfolds, we know that God is close to us humans, as close as our breath. God's spirit is in us, we are created in the image of God, and yet, we realize we are of the earth, the mud.

The garden itself was beautiful, verdant, and Adam could eat of any tree except the one in the middle—the tree of the knowledge of good and evil. The garden, however, is a lonely place, and just as Jahweh desires relationship with Adam, Adam also needs a companion of his own kind. It seems we humans are built for relationship, at least that is what this story teaches. Jahweh creates animals and birds, but no companion is adequate. Jahweh completes the creation finally with Eve. Adam now has a partner and human society—human community—is born. My own understanding of this story, and the Bible generally, was greatly enhanced when, as a twelve-year-old boy, I learned the word "Adam" in Hebrew also meant humanity. Without community and relationship, we are not fully human.

When the "J" story of creation is placed next to the "P" story we see God presented as close to us (immanent) and very distant (transcendent). It appears to be a contradiction, but it is also a blessing because it allows us to hold in tension two aspects of God's nature we humans have envisaged and experienced throughout history. The two stories complement each other and even though they contradict, they also balance our understanding of God's nature. It is, however, not only God's distance versus God's closeness that finds balance and completion here; there is also the question of evil. Both stories are essential to a new understanding of something called "theodicy"—the theological word for the problem of evil in our world.

The "J" writer speaks about the nearness of God but also about a question the "P" writer leaves unresolved. In the creation story of the priestly writers, God is all powerful, transcendent, and creates with a word and everything is good. It is a creation story different from all the other creation stories circulating in the ancient Near East. Usually creation myth stories included stories of a great struggle or battle between two opposing forces. The Babylonian Enuma

Elish creation story is an example. Marduk becomes the great hero of the Babylonian religion because he slew the powerful dragon Tiamat and then sliced her in two. He then used the two halves to create the sky and the earth. Obviously in this story, as with every other creation story in the Near East, the earth, the material world, has some evil embedded in it. The Hebrews told a story where there is only one God who is all powerful and creates the world to be only good. The question that remains then is, "Where does evil come from?"

When "J" tells his story of the garden, part of the purpose is to speak to the question of evil present in God's good world. As we mentioned "J" uses story to make a theological point. Therefore, "J" tells the story of Adam and Eve, a talking serpent, a fruit from the tree in the middle of the garden, and the dire consequences. The tree of the knowledge of good and evil is in the garden and Jahweh is careful to warn the humans not to eat from it, "for surely on that day you will die." Jahweh gave the humans the gift of limits, like a parent putting limits on children. A talking serpent (not Satan at this point in Scripture) then tempts Eve to eat of the fruit, Eve tempts Adam, and soon both have eaten and something within them has surely died. The relationship of openness, trust, honesty, and love which Jahweh had intended is replaced by deceit, blame, arrogance, and rebellion. Now Adam and Eve, whose openness had been symbolized by their nakedness, must cover themselves with a façade of competence symbolized by the clothing made of fig leaves.

By telling this story, the "J" writer completes the story of "P." The "J" writer, however, does not answer the question directly. Where does evil come from if God has created a good world? Well, it could be from the talking serpent, or maybe the woman, or the man. Evil may be a power outside the creation, and we humans may cooperate with that evil power, but the way the story is told we can't quite get a handle on who is to blame. The story leaves us uncertain about the origin of evil because the Bible has a higher purpose. By placing these stories side by side, we hold to the belief that God is good and creates a good world. We also acknowledge, however, that there is evil in this good world God has made. The "J" story is not so concerned about the origin of that evil; rather the "J" writer begins the biblical story by speaking to a different question—not where does evil come from but what does God do about the evil in God's good world. The remainder of the Bible, in fact, will be a description of God's response to the reality of sin, evil, and death in this paradise created by God.

Two theologians—"J" and "P"—are presented to the reader of the Genesis creation stories. They present their stories and their conceptions of God quite differently from the other, but those differences do not need to be softened or even harmonized. In fact, we must leave the differences hard and dramatic to hold in tension aspects of God which speak to our ideas about the divine. God is distant and close. God is all good but there is evil. God, and we ourselves, desire relationship but we turn from each other. We humans have the breath of God in us and we are fashioned from the earth. We have dreams of the infinite and, yet, are bound to the finite. All these are contradictions, blessed contradictions.

Contemporary Application

The contemporary debate between people who embrace evolutionary theory and those called "creationist" would be greatly altered if we understood the Genesis creation stories less as science and more as the Bible's way of describing the nature of God. When we treat the Genesis creation stories as scientific fact we miss the point of what the "J" and "P" writers have to teach us. In fact, people who advocate a "creationist" understanding of Genesis regarding how the world was created often will use scientific criteria to prove their points. Creationists will talk about the complexity of the nature and of life. They will attempt to discredit certain scientific tests but then use scientific criteria to prove a point which they believe supports creationism.

Evolutionists, on the other hand, will often roll their eyes at the creationists and take nothing at all from the creation stories in Genesis. What if we took the Genesis creation stories out of the realm of science and allowed them to speak to us about the nature of God and humanity? We could abandon trying to prove whether evolution or creationism is true because science and the Bible speak to two different questions. Science addresses the question how the world was created, and the Bible speaks about who and why the world is created. Would it not be wonderful to have all the people caught up in creationism instead turn their energies to studying all the creation stories of the ancient Near East and then compare them to the Genesis stories. They would learn that at the core of the Babylonia creation stories was a great monster that had to be defeated and the earth was made from the remnants of that monster. What does that say about the value and goodness of the creation? The Hebrews, in their creation story, said the world is good, not monstrous. The Greeks told creation stories which included betrayal, trickery, conflict, and strife. Again, what does that say about the nature of God and the nature of the creation? It is ultimately a dangerous place where you must use your wits and strength to survive. The Hebrews told creation stories that described the creation as a paradise and God deeply desiring peace, justice, and relationship. The Hebrew creations stories have so much more to teach us than scientific knowledge and the creationists today are diminishing the Bible by limiting its scope.

Discussion Questions

1. As you consider the nature of God, do you see God as "transcendent" or "immanent"? Is God as close to us as our breath, or so distant as to be wholly other? Share your personal story.

2. We tend to want to place blame for sin on Adam, Eve, or the snake. Does it matter? What difference does it make to think the Hebrew people were less concerned with blame and more with God's desire to nurture a positive human community?

3. Every culture has mythologies which celebrate and teach its greatest ideas and values. The Greeks told stories of heroism, bravery, conflict, and human ingenuity. The Egyptians, stories which encouraged societal stability. The Babylonians, stories of cosmic dangers and human insignificance. What great ideas and values did the Hebrew creation mythologies celebrate? How are they different from surrounding cultures?

4. What are some American mythological stories—factual or fiction—that we tell to promote values and ideas? What are some stories your family tells which promote the values you hold dear?

—— *Chapter Two* ——

Leviticus vs. the Prophets

IN CHAPTER 1 WE discussed two of the authors of the Genesis creation stories. The "Jahwist" and the "Priestly" writers present descriptions of God which are contradictory. The "J" writer describes God as close to us—intimate and relational—while to the "P" writers, God is distant, awesome, and beyond us. Each description, though different from the other, makes a valid point about what we believe to be the nature of God. Taken together the two stories are a blessed contradiction and help us better understand the divine.

The creation stories themselves not only describe the nature of God but also begin addressing some other significant theological issues. One of those issues is the theodicy question. If God creates the world good, why is there evil? Why is the world so broken? Who is to blame for evil? How can God's good world be reclaimed? How is "paradise" reinstated? As we concluded our look at the creation stories, we were confronted with a new way to look at these questions of evil and brokenness. Typically, we tend to emphasize and look for the *source* of evil in the world. We ask "Why?" and "Who's to blame?" The creation stories, however, leave those questions unanswered. We don't know who is really to blame—Adam? Eve? The serpent? Even God for planting the tree to begin with? The story does not deal with how or even why evil is in the world, instead the story is about what God does about the brokenness of the world. In some ways the entire Bible is God's way of putting the world together again and we are amazed at the method God will use. God will start small.

Following the creation stories in Genesis, the story of evil and brokenness begins to unfold, and we are shown how God responds. Following the creation stories in Genesis 1 through 3, we have the story of sin and evil affecting all of creation in chapters 4 through 11. Then in chapter 12, one of the most important chapters in the Bible, God begins the work of putting the world together in a most surprising way—God works from the bottom up. Instead of using grand gestures, power, or force, God deals with evil by calling two ordinary people—Abram and Sarai—to begin building a community of people which would be an example to the world of how God intends us to live. With their names changed, Abraham and Sarah have a hard time believing God can or will fulfill the three promises made to them. One, God promised to give them descendants as many as the stars of the sky. Yet, they do not have even one child. Two, God is going to give them a land in which they can live. Well, where is it? They were nomads following their sheep and goats. Three, God is going to bless the whole world through them. How can God mend the universe by starting so small—with these two minor players in history? Because we typically view God working from the top down—see God as powerful and able to change everything with a word—we usually ask questions like these when we are confronted with evil or tragedy. "Where was God? Why doesn't God do something?" God must be absent, incompetent, or uncaring. Rarely do we see the power and presence of the divine in small, hidden movements of people who bring justice, compassion, and peace to the world. Genesis chapter 12 teaches us that God is at work in the world through ordinary people from the bottom up.

The remainder of the book of Genesis and the first part of Exodus is the story of God's promises beginning to take shape. Abraham and Sarah do have descendants and, in time, a long time, they number a great multitude. One promise is fulfilled but there is no land in which they can live. Exodus is about the Hebrew descendants of Abraham and Sarah reaching a land of promise. They are liberated from their captivity in Egypt and follow a wilderness wandering; after a generation they were on the verge of entering a new land. The books of the Bible which describe the time in the wilderness—the second half of Exodus, Leviticus, and Numbers—are often biblical books we overlook. They seem concerned with rather petty rules and rituals—the size and shape of the Tent of Meeting, where the tribes should camp, and the proper way to make a sacrifice. There are also so many rules, not just the Ten Commandments, but rules about livestock wandering into another family's property or how it was not allowed to wear clothing made of two materials. What is the value of this part of the Bible? Why should we study it? How does it fit in to God's intention of putting the world together again?

It was during this wilderness wandering that we hear exclusively from one specific school of biblical writers—the priests. We have already heard from the priestly (P) writers when we studied the creation stories. They had presented God as powerful and distant from humanity, hence the need for priests to properly prepare methods of approaching such an awesome God. Now, in Exodus, Leviticus, and Numbers we hear the priests again, and now they emphasize the glue which will hold the new community together. They give us the Ten Commandments, the ritual Decalogue, and the many laws in Leviticus. They emphasize rules, rituals, and requirements which will give structure and guidance to the community God has brought together. The priests are keepers of the institutions of the new nation.

Central to the community was the torah—the law—the teaching. The Ten Commandments were known as the Decalogue—the ten words that would describe what a God-community would be like: no idols, no swearing, Sabbath worship, honor parents, no killing, no adultery, no stealing, no lying, no coveting of property or people. The Ten Commandments reflect well the (P) writer's emphasis on institution—living as God's community. As you may remember from the movie with Charlton Heston playing the part of Moses, there are two tablets of the Ten Commandments. As a child I always thought there were two tablets because God could not fit all the commandments on one stone. Silly me. Now I have learned that the first "tablet" contains commandments describing how we relate to God, and the second "tablet," those commandments related to people living in community. These two tablets form the basis for society—worship God, respectfully live with one another.

Upon the torah—the teaching—the priestly writers would build up the institutions by which the entire community of God's people would be held together. Institutions based on rules, rituals, traditions, and forms are vital to any community. It is true, of course, that any association of people needs structure. Think of the organizations to which you have belonged—schools, clubs, churches, political parties, fraternities, sororities, unions, cities, nations, etc.—all of them are institutions with rules as the glue which holds people together for a common purpose. The very rules which benefit and bind together groups of people, however, can also cause frustration. Rules that work well for one stage of an organization's life may not work well in the future. Institutions meant to serve the public good can become sclerotic and self-serving. There is always a tension between the institution as a stabilizing framework for an organization and the changing needs of that organization. Ideas for reform are often brought by individuals who challenge the institution; in the Bible we call these individual reformers prophets.

One of the most significant conflicts in the Bible is that between the Priestly writers and the prophets. The priests represent the "establishment"—the institution—while the prophets represent the voice of reform, even revolution. The priests seek to create and hold together the community of the chosen people with an emphasis on maintaining the institutions; the prophets seek to critique the structure of society and accomplish reform of the institutions. Biblical writers Isaiah, Jeremiah, and Ezekiel are the "major" prophets, so called because their works are simply longer than the writings or the "minor" prophets: Hosea, Joel, Amos, Obadiah, Jonah, Micah, Nahum, Habakkuk, Zephaniah, Haggai, Zechariah, and Malachi. The various prophetic writers have comments to make regarding their own unique situations, but they do hold in common a willingness, even a passion, to critique the institutions of their society, primarily the institutions of religion and state. The prophets critique the abuses of king and priest, calling for reform and a return to God's intentions. The prophets call for economic justice, political reform, and renewal of religious commitment, not just adherence to the formal requirements of the priestly leaders. The prophets and the priestly writers seem contradictory as one group seeks to maintain the institutions of society, while the other seeks to challenge or reform those institutions.

The tension evident between the priests and the prophets is significant enough that it could be called one of the Bible's most significant contradictions; it is, however, a blessed contradiction. God's intention for the chosen people, and for all of creation, is that there be a community and world of peace, justice, compassion, equity, grace, and love. God desires people to be connected to each other—hence the need for institutions, rules, requirements, form, and structure. Those structures, however, may need to adjust over time as the world changes; institutions must be flexible to serve new generations. One of the most significant challenges for the people who devised the American Constitution was to create a structure—a government that would be stable—and also allow for change. Our Founding Fathers addressed that inherent contradiction with the possibility of amending the Constitution. The Bible addresses the same tension between stability and change with the work of the priests and that of the prophets.

In my own career as a pastor, I experience the contradiction and tension evident in the priestly writers versus the prophetic writers. The "priestly" function of a pastor is to maintain the forms and structures of the church. The church is an institution with rules, rituals, and requirements needed to bind a community of people together. Budgets, committee meetings, and liturgical planning may not seem to be profound parts of ministry, yet without attention to the needs of the institution there would soon be no proclamation of God's message and no community of people seeking to live together as God intends.

People will sometimes say they do not need to go to church to be Christian. Churches have so many deficiencies. They are at times corrupt, stuck in the past, and out of touch with the world. People think they don't need to be part of such an institution; maybe so, but does not God throughout the Bible seek to nurture community? Doesn't God seek to put the world together again by empowering groups of people to live in harmony? Is that not the purpose of the promises to Abraham and Sarah? Is not living together in harmony what the priests and the prophets were all about? Did not Jesus seek to create a community and not simply a following of individual believers separate from each other and the world? The contradiction between the priestly writers and the prophets shows us the biblical emphasis on the institution, the community of believers.

The prophets never sought to destroy institutions, rather they desired to reform them. Many pastors also have the prophetic desire to bring about reform to churches, schools, government, but pastors must also simultaneously maintain the institutions that give form and structure to God's community. It can be frustrating to be caught in the tension—the contradiction—between maintaining the form and structure of institutions and calling for reform and change. Yet, there is a blessing in this tension. We recognize the need for the conserving function of the priests, and we can see the need for the prophets to seed continual reform. The roles of priest and prophet are both important and essential for a healthy community. The blessed contradiction between working to maintain the institution and critiquing the same institution are parts of every Christian's spiritual journey and responsibility. On one hand, we maintain the forms and the rituals of the past and, on the other, we challenge and change those forms to more closely adhere to God's intention. It is a process without end and a blessed contradiction in our faith. We are all priests and prophets and we must balance the tension inherent in those two roles. The Bible highlights this blessed contradiction in the tension between Leviticus and the prophets.

Discussion Questions

1. Leviticus and other parts of Scripture which are often referred to as "the law," have often been viewed as rules to control, or even crush, human striving. Yet, "the law" represents the biblical attempt to institutionalize the godly desire to create and foster a righteous human community. What are some of the positive aspects of "the law?" How was/is the institution of the religious system beneficial? How was/is it harmful?

2. Consider modern institutions. Name some. What is the purpose of these institutions? How can they become too restrictive, even oppressive?

3. Old Testament prophets are unanimous in their purpose—they all criticize institutions, cultural norms, and personal behavior antithetical to God's desires for justice, compassion, and peace. If "the law" represents stability and tradition, the prophets represent a movement, even revolution. Name some modern prophets who have offered critique of the institutions and social structures in our world. Discuss the difference between a movement and an institution. Consider the American Revolution as a movement and the Constitution as the beginning of an institution.

4. We all live with certain worldviews—frameworks by which we give our lives meaning and purpose. They are our personal "institutions," if you will, and they include our religious beliefs or nonbelief, our political opinions and our ethical norms. When has your "worldview" been challenged and who was the "prophet" who offered critique?

—— *Chapter Three* ——

Deuteronomy vs. Job

IN CHAPTER 1 WE considered the two creation stories present in the book of Genesis. The "Jahwist" writer described God as immanent—as close to us as our heartbeat. The "Priestly" writers described God as transcendent or distant, beyond us, other. In chapter 2 we saw the Bible begin to deal with God's method of putting a broken world back together. God would work from the bottom up through common people like Abraham and Sarah . . . and through ordinary people like us. It was God's intention to reclaim the "paradise" intended for the creation by building a community—a people worshipping God and living together in a caring, just community. We saw that inherent in creating community were rules, rituals, and requirements—forms which continually need critique and reform. Here we met two sets of writers that seem to be contradictory. The priests maintained the institutions and the prophets challenged those institutions. Both groups— priests and prophets—had a role to play and we came to see that the contradiction could be truly a blessing.

Now we are ready to consider another contradiction; this one between the group of theologians responsible for Deuter- onomy and the ones responsible for Job. Although the theo- logical perspectives of these two theological schools are many and quite diverse, we will here consider one issue, the issue of theodicy. Theodicy, as mentioned in chapter 2, is the question of evil in God's good world. The creation stories introduce us to this subject with the story of a talking serpent, Adam, Eve, God walking in the garden, disobedience, punishment, and anguish. Evil enters the creation. The story never does fully explain the source or the reason for evil; is it the serpent's fault? Eve? Adam? Or even God for creating the tree in the middle of the garden in the first place? As we noted earlier, the Genesis stories of creation chose not to assign blame or to give us a reason for evil; rather Genesis sets us up to consider the far more important question: What does God do about the evil and brokenness in our world?

It seems, however, that biblical writers just could not resist the temptation to assign blame for evil. The Deuteronomist writers were so concerned about such issues that they proceeded to retell the whole story of God's people. In fact, the word "Deuteronomy" literally means a second telling of the law. Each generation of God's people was to hear and experience God's commitment and respond to it and, depending upon the response, blessings or curses would follow. If bad things happened to you it was because you did something to deserve them and if good things came your way it was because you were living according to God's intention. The Deuteronomist's answer to the theodicy question was black and white. Evil things happen because you are being cursed by God. Good things happen because God is rewarding you. Deuteronomy 28 beginning at verse 1 reads: "And if you obey the voice of the Lord your God, being careful to do all his commandments which I command you this day, the LORD your God will set you high above all the nations of the earth. And all these blessings shall come upon you and overtake you, if you obey the voice of the LORD your God. Blessed shall you be in the city, and blessed shall you be in the field. Blessed shall be the fruit of your body, and the fruit of your ground, and the fruit of your beasts, the increase of your cattle, and the young of your flock. Blessed shall be your basket and your kneading-trough. Blessed shall you be when you come in, and blessed shall you be when you go out."

In the same chapter, just a few verses later the Deuter-onomist writes about curses. Verse 15 and following reads: "But if you will not obey the voice of the LORD your God or be careful to do all his commandments and his statutes which I command you this day, then all these curses shall come upon you and overtake you. Cursed shall you be in the city, and cursed shall you be in the field. Cursed shall be your basket and your kneading-trough. Cursed shall be the fruit of your body, and the fruit of your ground, the increase of your cattle and the young of your flock. Cursed shall you be when you come in, and cursed shall you be when you go out. The Lord will send upon you curses, confusion, and frustration, in all that you undertake to do, until you are destroyed and perish quickly, on account of the evil of your doings, because you have forsaken me."

On the most surface level, it is possible to see some truth in the Deuteronomist theodicy. If we live lives that are healthy, balanced, holistic, and godly, things often go well for us. If we embrace the Ten Commandments and strive for a life of virtue, we are often rewarded with happiness. If we eat right, avoid smoking, and get some daily exercise good things often follow. There is some level of truth then to the theodicy of the Deuteronomist but it is a theology obviously in need of critique.

The Bible brings such a critique of Deuteronomy in the message of the book of Job. Job is a book from a part of the Bible called the wisdom literature and is a story familiar to many people who have not even read the Bible. Job is a wealthy, happy, and faithful man who seems to be enjoying the fruits of his faith. Because he has followed God's law he has been richly blessed; it is exactly the theology of Deuteronomy. As the story continues to unfold Satan is talking with God and, to paraphrase, basically says, *Job is only faithful because you, God, are giving him such rich rewards. Job is faithful because of what he gets out of it. Take away his blessings, God, and Job will no longer be faithful.* The writer of Job is telling a story which directly challenges the theology and theodicy of the Deuteronomist. According to Job, it is just too simple to say that following the covenant always brings blessings and breaking the covenant always brings curse. We, of course, would make the same critique. We all know people who suffer through no fault of their own and people who prosper unethically.

The story of Job then continues to tell a story of a faithful man who loses everything—wealth, family, health, happiness—all are gone. In his despair, Job is sent counselors to console him and each spouts out some form of the Deuteronomist theodicy. "Job you must have done something wrong to suffer all these curses." "Job, just think back and remember what you did and then repent." "Job, you can't be innocent. God blesses the innocent and curses the guilty. You must be guilty." Chapter after chapter the counselors hammer home this old theology. Even Job lives within the framework of the Deuteronomist theodicy. "I did nothing wrong, God, why do you punish me?" "It's not fair, God, we had a deal." Finally, God speaks out of a whirlwind and tells

Job, "Shut up and listen." Or words to that effect. "Who are you to ask me questions? Do you understand all things?" God challenges the very premise of the theodicy question. Even asking the theodicy question—why bad things happen to good people?—assumes the idea that the world ought to be fair and God ought to reward good behavior, and bad things should not happen to us if we behave. Job challenges that human assumption by placing these words in the mouth of God from chapter 40, verse 6, "Then the LORD answered Job out of the whirlwind: 'Gird up your loins like a man; I will question you, and you declare to me. Will you even put me in the wrong? Will you condemn me that you may be justified?'" Suddenly Job (and hopefully the reader) has a revelation. The theodicy question is reoriented. No longer do we focus on why bad things happen to good people. No longer do we remain faithful because we are promised some rich blessing. Instead, the question becomes: In the face of an uncertain and erratic universe where good and bad come our way in life, what is our response? Do we choose to embrace an understanding of reality with a divine center yearning for wholeness and joy; or do we continue to put ourselves at the center demanding fairness and/or reward.

Job now changes his approach. Instead of demanding that God be fair, he simply says, in chapter 42, verse 5, "I had heard of thee by the hearing of the ear, but now my eye sees thee; therefore I am humbled and repent in dust and ashes." The Bible uses the word "repent" but the real Hebrew word meaning is closer to "melt." Job "melts" before God, and ultimately realizes the theodicy question is too big for him. Theodicy may also be too much for us. We don't know why evil things happen and we really don't need to know. The book of Job invites us to look honestly at the blessings and curses this world has to offer and choose to humbly place ourselves in reverent faith that God is still present to us and to the entire creation.

Contemporary Application

In past centuries Christian preachers often used the threat of God's wrath to motivate believers. Descriptions of the torments of hell were included in sermons, literature, and works of art. Johann Tetzel, the seller of indulgences who was opposed by Martin Luther, once gave a sermon that included thrusting his own hand into a flame until it blistered. With wide, threatening eyes, he showed his hand to the congregation and warned them hell would be an eternity of this kind of pain. Dante wrote a powerful poetic description of hell in his work called the *Inferno*. His graphic images have been common to Christianity ever since. Statues and stained glass windows in medieval cathedrals often portrayed those suffering in hell. The curse of hell was very real.

The Deuteronomist theologians would have applauded the use of hellfire to motivate people to faithfulness; it fit perfectly with their theology. Those who follow God's law are blessed and those who break God's law are cursed. If you have not put yourself right with God, ultimately the curse of hell will follow. Today many Christians continue to live with this understanding of the afterlife, although it is rare to hear preachers harangue their congregations about the torments of hell. It is much more likely that a congregation will hear the other half of the Deuteronomist blessing/curse theology. Remember that breaking the law will bring curses but following the law will bring blessings. Usually we understand the ultimate blessing to be going to heaven after we die, but recently preachers across America have been proclaiming a message called the "prosperity" gospel. The "prosperity" gospel takes the theology of the Deuteronomist and makes it contemporary to a world focused on material well-being. The "prosperity" gospel preachers promise good things—blessings—in this world to all those who do what the preacher considers essential—following the law, having a born-again experience, making a contribution, voting the right way, or speaking in tongues. The blessings of the prosperity gospel can include better health, advancement in one's career, finding a job, getting a relationship, or handling one's debt, etc.

Although we can obviously see the "prosperity" gospel as shallow theology, it does have some truth to it. Often people who turn to a spiritual life will begin overcoming many of the obstacles which have held them back and blessings can follow. The Deuteronomist theologians do have a message to share; the threat of hell can be real and the promise of heaven, or even the prosperity on earth, can be an important part of a spiritual journey. However, if we embrace only the Deuteronomist theology and not balance it with the message of Job, we will get only a shallow, either-or, black-and-white understanding of what the Bible teaches us about blessings and curses. Indeed, this shallow theology was evident when the threat of hell dominated Christianity in the past and we see it when the promise of prosperity entices people today. The writer of Job offers a contradiction and a correction to the Deuteronomist; it could even be called a blessed contradiction for it deepens and balances our understanding of the blessings and curses that come our way. Blessings do not always follow faithfulness and curses do not always follow bad behavior. Do we have faith in a benevolent God anyway? Job would say, yes.

Discussion Questions

1. The question of suffering in God's good world is called "theodicy," and it is concerned with why we suffer and for what purpose. The theologians of the Deuteronomistic school proposed that blessings come to those who follow God's law and curses (and suffering) come to those who do not. Give examples from your own life how you have understood and experienced the theodicy question in a similar way as the Deuteronomist.

2. Can you give examples how the Deuteronomist writers are sometimes correct? Give examples that do not include a religious viewpoint.

3. Job, famously, is a book about a good and righteous man who, nonetheless, endures great suffering. How is Job a significant contradiction to the ideas of the Deuteronomist? Share your own examples of unjust suffering.

4. What can we do with the question of suffering? Give examples of how we might reframe suffering differently than the Deuteronomist's emphasis on suffering as punishment.

─── *Chapter Four* ───

Ezra/Nehemiah vs. Ruth/Jonah

THE BOOKS OF EZRA and Nehemiah are written in the tradition of the Deuteronomist theology and describe events in the history of Israel following something called the Babylonian exile. The Babylonian exile followed many centuries of Israel struggling with its relationship with God. Israel came into existence as a people with its own land after Moses led the Hebrews out of Egypt probably sometime around 1250 BCE. After forty years in the wilderness, Joshua led the Hebrew people into Canaan where they conquered and infiltrated the land and established a loosely organized confederation of twelve tribes. For nearly two hundred years the twelve tribes lived without a king ruling a centralized government, but with neighboring countries growing stronger, the Hebrews decided to choose a king about the year 1040 BCE. His name was Saul and he molded the twelve tribes into a nation with a strong army and a centralized government; his dynasty, however, would not last. King David followed Saul and then it was David's son Solomon's turn. At Solomon's death in 922 BCE the kingdom split in two—the ten northern tribes would be called Israel and the two southern tribes would be known as Judah. The two countries existed side by side, worshipped the same God, until in 722 BCE the ten northern tribes—Israel—were destroyed by the Assyrian Empire and were forever lost to history. A little more than a century later a new empire, Babylon, rose to power and defeated the Assyrians. The Babylonians now dominated the ancient Near East and in 587 BCE Judah, the southern kingdom, was conquered and many of the people were deported to the city of Babylon but they would not be lost to history as the ten northern tribes had been. The Jews who were captive in the Babylonian exile maintained their faith and identity as a community and waited for the day they would return to their homeland, which they did after the Persian Empire defeated the Babylonians in 539 BCE. The Persians had an enlightened policy of encouraging the people in their empire to build their own temples, have their own kings, and maintain their unique traditions. The books of Ezra (a priest) and Nehemiah (a political leader) are the history of this postexilic period, a period when a new blessed contradiction arose within the reestablished Jewish community.

Imagine the joy of the Jewish people when they learned they would be permitted to return to their homeland after nearly fifty years in Babylonian exile. You would think there would be a frantic dash to return and rebuild Jerusalem, the temple, and the economy of Judah, but there was no such enthusiasm. The Jews had become well established in Babylon and many of them were prospering quite well and to return to Judah would involve a thousand-mile journey and starting life over. A certain contingent of people, however, did find the courage and fortitude to make the return and once they did, they were confronted with many problems. The temple needed rebuilding, the walls of Jerusalem had been torn down, the economy was in shambles, and many strangers were now living in the land.

The presence of strangers was the biggest surprise. Many of these strangers were people who claimed to worship the same God as the Jews, but they were not part of the ethnic Jewish community. Often called Samaritans, these strangers were dangerous, or so the Jews thought. If the returning exiles began to marry the strangers living in the land soon the ethnic identity of the nation would be diminished. The post-exile issue for the Jews is one that has affected communities of people throughout history. How does a group maintain its uniqueness in a diverse society? What are the factors that determine one's membership in a group? Is it exclusive to set up criteria for membership? Is some form of exclusivity essential to the identity of a group? What does it mean then to be inclusive? What is the balance between exclusivity and inclusiveness? In the case of the postexilic Jews, the emphasis of the religious and political leaders was heavily in favor of the exclusive.

When Ezra, the priest, arrived in Judah, earlier returning exiles had begun settling into their new life with the strangers they met. In fact, many Jews had inter-married and some were even intrigued by the religious traditions of their new wives or husbands. Ezra was appalled! If the people of Judah kept up this fraternization with the locals, there would soon be no Jewish nation and no Jewish religion. In Ezra's mind, he had to put a stop to all this intermarriage and he had to exert religious intolerance toward anyone who believed anything different from orthodox Jewish thought. In Ezra chapter 10, verse 10, the priest, Ezra, stood before a crowd of Jewish men and pointed his finger. "You have trespassed and married foreign women, and so increased the guilt of Israel. Now then make confession to the LORD the God of your fathers, and do his will; separate yourselves

from the peoples of the land and from the foreign wives."
It was a sad day for those foreign wives because the Jewish
men did exactly as Ezra instructed and more; they also cast
out of the community all the children born to those mixed
marriages. There would be no mixed blood people in the
newly restored Judah. The chosen people of God embraced
exclusion to keep themselves pure.

Nehemiah reinforced the exclusivity of the priest Ezra
in the political arena. Nehemiah was the governor of the
new Persian Empire's province of Judah and he was free to
run things as he saw fit. As a good Jew himself, Nehemiah
was aware of the same problem Ezra noticed. The chosen
people were mixing too freely with the diverse population
they found in Judah upon their return from exile. Ezra im-
posed religious rules on the Jews, and now Nehemiah would
impose political and economic rules. It was almost as if Ezra
and Nehemiah were walling the Jewish people off from the
surrounding people and, considering Nehemiah's leadership,
this was literally true. Nehemiah's priority was to rebuild the
walls surrounding Jerusalem. It was a controversial decision
because many of the local people were quite offended. "Why
do you need walls?" "Just let people come and go." "We have
gotten along quite well for fifty years without walls." "In fact,
it is a good thing that everyone can mix together." Nehemiah
responded with these exclusive words from chapter 2, verse
20. "Then I replied to them, 'The God of heaven will make
us [and not you] prosper, and we his servants, will arise and
build; but you have no portion or right or memorial in Jerusalem.'" Jerusalem would be for the Jews and the walls would
keep the communities separate just as Ezra's religious rules
kept the religions separate.

A few years ago, our church sponsored a trip to Israel, and we had the opportunity to cross a modern wall separating Israelis from Palestinians. Although it has been nearly 2,500 years since Nehemiah erected his walls, his words excluding the locals from the chosen people could have been uttered today. As we made our way through a checkpoint and gate in the modern wall, teenage Israeli soldiers in guard towers peered down on us and intense bureaucrats examined our passports. Once in the Palestinian area we met residents of a refugee camp; they had lived in their squalid conditions since the 1948 war. The refugees told us the wall was an offense and would never lead to a permanent peace. A permanent peace must be the result of honest and respectful dialogue not the building of exclusive walls. "They must stop treating us like outcasts!" was a sentence that still rings in our ears.

Ezra, the priest, and Nehemiah, the governor, used exclusion to protect and unify the Jewish nation. They feared the dilution and economic insecurity diversity might bring and so erected their walls of separation to keep others out. We look at what they did, and it appears too harsh and intolerant; their exclusivity needs critique. The Bible indeed does bring such a critique in the message of books like Ruth and Jonah. These books contradict the exclusive emphasis of the Deuteronomist theologians who wrote Ezra and Nehemiah but before we consider Ruth and Jonah, it is important to look at the positive side of exclusive theology.

"Exclusive" has become a politically incorrect word these days but we should remember every group we belong to exerts some form of exclusion. There are identifying factors which set apart every group. These factors can be biological, racial, economic, religious, political, or social. The scouting programs have rules and guidelines which determine membership. A girl or boy voluntarily adheres to these rules and participates with others who also join the organizations. The children feel part of something bigger than themselves and they begin to grow into adulthood. Most people would say this kind of exclusivity is positive and essential if there are going to be any groupings of people striving together for a good purpose. Service clubs, such as Rotary or Kiwanis, welcome all interested people, however, there is an expectation of participation and working with others in the group. On one level, this is exclusive because not all people would be considered Rotarians or Kiwanians. Is there not something positive about a group that welcomes all but has expectations for those who choose to affiliate and strive for good works?

Many examples abound of the need for human beings to come together in groups for security, service, personal growth, or to accomplish some project too big for an individual. Those who choose not to participate in such groupings are excluded. Exclusion becomes negative when an attitude of arrogance develops within a group. When we talk about "us versus them" or stereotype all members of a certain group we begin making exclusion negative. The writers of Ezra and Nehemiah took the proper need for exclusion too far. All the negative aspects of exclusivity are evident in these books—arrogance, insensitivity, fear, and inflexibility. It is like a pendulum that has swung too far in one direction, in this case an extreme exclusivity. The Bible, however, brings the pendulum back from the extreme and in the case of postexilic exclusivity there are books that contradict the theology of the Deuteronomist.

The books of Ruth and Jonah are often read and studied independent of their place in the overall sweep of biblical theology. Ruth is taught as a lesson in faithfulness—we should be as faithful as Ruth was to her mother-in-law. "Where you go, I will go. Where you lodge, I will lodge" (Ruth 1:16). Jonah often begins a debate about the impossibility of a person being swallowed by a huge fish and we get no further into the meaning of the story than that. Seen in the context of the entire Bible, however the books of Ruth and Jonah become a response to the exclusivity of the Deuteronomist.

The story of Ruth begins with Elimelech and Naomi with their two sons leaving Judah during a time of famine seeking prosperity in the neighboring country of Moab. While in Moab, Elimelech dies and Naomi is left with her two sons, who proceed to marry Moabite women, but the sons, like their father, also die. Naomi is left with two daughters-in-law and no men. Because Naomi decides to return to Judah, the daughters-in-law could certainly have stayed in their home country of Moab, but one of them—Ruth—decides to stay with Naomi. It is at this point in the story that Ruth declares, "Where you go, I will go, where you lodge, I will lodge. Your God will be my God." The story then proceeds to describe the life and the virtue of Ruth as she cares for Naomi. Ruth marries a wealthy Jewish man and is a paragon of virtue— the kind of person God would intend for any of his chosen people . . . and that's the hook in the story. She is not one of the chosen people, she is an outsider, a Moabite, the other, and yet no one could deny she is one of God's own. The point of the story is that the outsider is one of us. Virtue, commitment, faith, kindness are the identifying factors which determine the participation in the community of God's chosen people. God's community is inclusive for any and all people who desire to step into it and Ruth, a Moabite, was one such person who took that step. The book of Ruth helps complete what could be greatly misunderstood in the theology of the Deuteronomist. The community of God's people is not defined as an ethnic group, or even by a set of religious doctrines, but rather by anyone who steps into the love, joy, peace, and grace God offers.

The book of Jonah, like Ruth, has been marginalized in the sweep of biblical theology precisely because it has been read in isolation from the rest of the Bible and especially from the work of the Deuteronomists. The story of Jonah and the big fish is what Jewish writers call a "haggadah," which is a tale that conveys some deep truths but may not be a literal story. The Jonah story can be read and understood on many levels, but too often we read it and remember only the big fish swallowing Jonah, but it is so much more.

The story of Jonah is the story of a reluctant prophet who resists God's call. Jonah was told by God to go to the city of Nineveh, the capital of the Assyrian Empire, and call on the people there to repent from their evil ways and God would forgive and bless them. The Assyrians were absolutely hated by everyone in the ancient Near East. Their cruelty and injustice were legendary and many people today have compared them to the Nazis of World War II. Jonah refused God's call precisely because he did not want the Assyrians to repent. He did not want God to forgive them. He did not want them as part of God's community. They were the "other" and Jonah loved to hate them.

Jonah boarded a ship bound for Spain, the direction that would take him as far as possible from God's call. His actions speak to our own tendency to often go in the direction opposite God's intention. As Jonah's ship sails, a great storm arises, symbolic, I suppose, of the storms that arise in our own lives when we travel in unhealthy directions.

Jonah is cast off the ship and sinks down into the depths of the sea and would have been lost except for the big fish God sends to scoop him up and regurgitate him back on land in the direction of Nineveh. In the twelve-step programs this is called the "bottoming out" before the healing can begin. Off Jonah now goes, traveling three days into the heart of the city of Nineveh. At the center of the city, he continues to be reluctant to preach to the Assyrians, so he says in a whisper, "Repent and God will forgive." Immediately the entire city repents in "sackcloth and ashes" and God indeed does forgive. Jonah, still unhappy, realizes that God will receive even the people the rest of the world would condemn.

There is no evidence in history to suggest that anything in the haggadah story of Jonah is literally true. Certainly, the Assyrians never did repent of their aggressive ways; they were finally and utterly crushed by a new empire, the Babylonians, and were lost to history. The point of telling the story then is seen in the context of the sweep of the biblical narrative, and especially in contradiction to the Deuteronomist writers of Ezra and Nehemiah who divided the world so sharply into us versus them. Jonah tells us the worst of "them" are loved by God. God does not seek to save only God's chosen few but rather to include and save all people. Jonah is a story of an inclusive theology that is directly opposed to the exclusive theology of the postexilic period and a book that is a blessing as it balances and completes the biblical theology of that period.

Discussion Questions

1. Ezra, a religious leader, and Nehemiah, a political leader, sought to reestablish a Jewish community in Israel following release from the Babylonian captivity in 586 BCE. They were exclusive in many ways, e.g., forbade intermarriage with non-Jews, built walls around Jerusalem, and cast out any people, including children, who were not ethnically pure. Give historic and modern examples of leaders establishing a unified community using exclusive methods.

2. Throughout history people tend to associate with others who are like themselves. What are some positive things resulting from this tendency? What are some negatives?

3. Ruth was a Moabite but also the ancestor of King David. Jonah was called to reach out to the Assyrians, the enemies of Israel. How are these two books contradictions to the exclusivity of Ezra and Nehemiah? Was their indirect challenge effective? Are there modern examples?

4. State ways you or your community have been exclusive. State ways you have reached out to the "other," that is, people outside your group.

Part Two

Blessed Contradictions: New Testament

JUST AS IN THE Old Testament, the New Testament has numerous authors and different types of literature—history, letters, sermons, and apocalyptic writing. The four gospels— Matthew, Mark, Luke, and John—which begin the New Testament were not the only "gospels" written. Dozens of gospels describing Jesus' life were written but only four were canonized (accepted) as sufficiently orthodox. The gospels of Thomas, Mary Magdalene, Judas, and many more told the Jesus story from unique theological perspectives, and so too did Matthew, Mark, Luke, and John. Mark was the first of the NT gospel writers and he shares a simply written, action-oriented account which ends without a record of the resurrection. Mark's emphasis was on the cross and Jesus' identification with human suffering and death. This *theology of the cross* was balanced by the perspective of John's gospel. John's *theology of glory* emphasized Jesus' power, control, and triumph over death. The Gospel of Matthew was especially written for a Jewish audience and presented Jesus as a new Moses, a new teacher of the torah. The Gospel of Luke, written for the Gentiles, emphasized Jesus as healer and builder of an inclusive community. The various ways the gospel writers told the story of Jesus' life appear contradictory, but by understanding the authors' special emphases they become a blessing helping the biblical reader get a more complete picture of who Jesus was and what his story means.

The remaining books of the New Testament are also written by authors who have theological points to make and sometimes these points seem to contradict each other. For example, in the Letter to the Romans, the Apostle Paul writes that human beings are "justified by faith apart from works of the law" (Rom 3:28). The book of James says the opposite, "a person is justified by works and not by faith alone" (Jas 2:24). Which is it? We don't have to choose. These contradictions can exist side by side when we consider the perspective and context of each of the writers. Again, allowing the contradictions to stand can enhance our understanding. A final contradiction we will consider is eschatology. The word "eschatology" means the study of the last things—the end times. Scripture presents a view that the end times will involve a last judgment and a separation of the saved and the lost. An alternative vision of the end times, however, is also present in the New Testament. It is the vision, rarely emphasized, of an inclusive heaven where all humanity and all creation are redeemed. In the following chapters we will consider these various visions of Mark versus John, Matthew versus Luke, Paul versus James, and exclusive versus inclusive end times.

—— *Chapter Five* ——

Mark's Theology of the Cross vs. John's Theology of Glory

THE GOSPEL OF MARK with its theology of the cross is an obvious contradiction to John's theology of glory, yet, both are true and both, helpful. In order to compare the two, it is important to consider each as a complete narrative and not simply a series of short passages (pericopes) as we often hear them in church worship services. Mark and John had a story to tell and each carefully arranged their material with a theological purpose in mind. To fully appreciate their theologies it is, therefore, important to get an overview of the way they tell the story, the narrative, of Jesus.

Mark is considered the earliest gospel to be written and, with sixteen chapters, it is also the shortest. Mark does not have a record of Jesus' birth nor a story of the resurrection. (Please note most Bibles today have two alternate endings to Mark, both of which were added later and were not part of the original story.) Mark writes his short, abrupt account of Jesus' life as a mystery story. We, the readers, are presented with an introduction to Jesus as if we had never heard of him. Mark's gospel was intended for an audience reading about Jesus for the first time and Mark uses a brilliant literary technique to grasp his reader's attention.

In the first half of the gospel (through ch. 8) Mark slowly reveals hints about Jesus' identity—Jesus heals, casts out demons, forgives sins, and calms the water. The hints build like a musical crescendo reaching for a climax. Beginning quietly, the small insights into Jesus' identity build until in chapter 8 we have a cymbal crash when Jesus asks his disciples, "Who do you say that I am?" Peter answers, "You are the Christ!" (Mark 8:29); and it seems we have the answer to the mystery. Mark's story, however, continues and we are taught what it means that Jesus is the Christ. In the second half of the gospel we expect the crescendo to continue as Jesus exerts his power as the Christ, the Messiah. Instead, we are surprised by a decrescendo as Jesus seems powerless and ends up crucified on Good Friday while a Roman centurion, of all people, looks on and proclaims, "Truly, this man is the Son of God" (Mark 15:39). Jesus' identity is finally revealed at the cross.

The mystery story which is the Gospel of Mark begins in chapter 1, verse 1, "The beginning of the good new of Jesus Christ, the Son of God." The phrase "Son of God," however, is not found in the earliest manuscripts and is considered by many scholars as added to the original. (A footnote in many Bibles explains the point.) The only other time Jesus is referred to as "Son of God" is by the demons who seem to know Jesus' identity throughout the narrative. The disciples are slow to grasp who Jesus is and their uncertainty is meant to match that of the original readers who, as mentioned, are being introduced to Jesus for the first time. The disciples and the reader will now be given a crescendo of hints as the gospel narrative unfolds.

One of the first clues comes at Jesus' baptism (Mark 1:9–11). At his baptism we hear God quote two passages from the

Old Testament, "You are my Son, the beloved," which comes from Psalm 2:7, an enthronement psalm used when a leader was anointed king. The hint then, of course, is Jesus must be a king; he is anointed at his baptism. We are surprised when a second quote comes from Isaiah 42:11, "With you I am well-pleased." We are surprised because Isaiah 42 is about a servant who suffers for the sake of others. Jesus, then, is both a king and one who suffers—an interesting juxtaposition and rather confusing for the reader.

Jesus' first words recorded in Mark 1:15 also hint at this identity, as well as his purpose, "The time is fulfilled, the kingdom of God has come near, repent and believe in the good news." Jesus' focus here is not so much about himself but about his purpose, which is to announce the kingdom of God—the society of grace, justice, and peace—is near or, as literally translated, is "at hand." The holy community, the just society, was as close as your hand. Look for it! Repent and believe! Repent means to turn from something and go in a different direction. In this case, to turn from the kingdom/society of injustice, violence, and greed. "Believe" is to turn toward something, in this case, the good news that the holy, just, and peaceable kingdom is near. The good and holy life is as close as your hand. Step into it. It is interesting that in this mystery story as to Jesus' identity, Jesus takes the focus off himself and invites the reader to enter the kingdom of God—to trust the good news that God's kingdom is close.

Following this dramatic opening where Mark shows Jesus' purpose, we quickly return to the mystery story, but now we also see Jesus' introducing some interesting people to this godly kingdom. He begins by calling his disciples; they are ordinary people, not scholars or priests. Jesus casts out demons like an exorcist. Jesus heals the sick and includes them in the kingdom. Is he a healer? An exorcist? Jesus heals a leper by reaching out his hand and touching the leper! We remember that the kingdom of God is as close as one's hand. Does this mean that in God's kingdom no one is "unclean?" In chapter 2 Jesus heals a paralytic and says, "Your sins are forgiven." Is Jesus taking over the role of the priests? Is the kingdom of God different from the religious institutions? Does God work outside the structures of religion? We readers are intrigued by this Jesus and so we read on.

When we arrive at chapter 4, Jesus begins to tell parables. It appears he is also a teacher, a rabbi. Jesus' parables, however, are not about himself but about the kingdom of God—that holy community which is close at hand but often unnoticed. Jesus says the kingdom—the holy community—is like a seed—small at first but when it finds fertile soil it grows to produce great and abundant fruits, like justice, kindness, and peace. The kingdom is like a lamp meant to shine into every dark corner, every lonely soul. The kingdom is meant to shine into the world like a lamp that brightens a dark room.

By the time we get to chapters 5 and 6, we are starting to get a picture of Jesus. Jesus is opening us to the kingdom of God—to God's intention for humanity and the created order. That kingdom, we discover in these chapters, is not limited to or defined by national, ethnic, or even religious identity. In Mark 4:35 Jesus says, "Let us go across to the other side." He means the "other side" of the Sea of Galilee which is a non-Jewish area called the Decapolis. Jesus and his disciples will be going to a foreign land and meeting alien people. We often think this chapter is about the storm on the water and how Jesus miraculously calms it with a word. Of course, when the wind and the sea obey Jesus' voice, a good first-century reader would immediately have thought of the creation story in Genesis when God spoke a word and the waters of chaos receded. The clue to Jesus' identity is that Jesus too pushes back the chaos to create the kingdom, the holy community.

The symbolism of a violent storm which nearly prevented Jesus and the disciples from reaching the "other side" is obvious. The "other side" represents all those not part of the "in group." Consider all the storms in society which accompany reaching out to the "other." Consider the storms which accompany change, especially change which brings greater equality, justice, and peace. Jesus pushes back the storm so that he can reach to the other side where he will heal a foreigner—the Gerasene demoniac. A woman of great faith, also a foreigner, simply touches the hem of Jesus' garment and is healed. Repenting and believing, the kingdom was certainly and literally "at hand" for her. Jairus's daughter had died but Jesus gently brings her to life. Maybe Jesus was talking about more than crossing the Galilee to foreign territory when he said, "Let us go to the other side." We often talk about death as going to the "other side." Here we read that the kingdom of God includes not only foreigners, the stranger, and the alien, but also those who have died. The kingdom of God—the holy community—had no barriers, no walls, and not even death can exclude us.

Following Jesus' outreach to the Decapolis—the "other side"—he returned home, to the people of Nazareth, where he met a storm of rejection. The people of Nazareth said he was only Jesus, Mary's son, what's so special about him? The good news of God's kingdom was so close to them, as close as their hands, as close as their neighbor, but they were not able to see it. Rejected, Jesus returned to the "other side," to the outsiders and the foreigners, the hungry and the poor.

He fed a great crowd of five thousand with five loaves of bread and two fish (Mark 6:30–44). It is often considered the miracle of multiplication but it was really a miracle of the spirit—here was an example of the kingdom of God where everyone had enough, where there were no barriers, and Jesus was at the center.

Now, finally, we have reached the midpoint of the Gospel of Mark. We are at a crescendo of clues as to Jesus' identity and we think we know who Jesus is—a healer, exorcist, priest, rabbi, teacher, and messiah. He is the leader of a new, holy, inclusive kingdom, a holy society. The disciples also thought they knew the answer to the mystery of Jesus' identity. At least Peter thought he knew. Mark 8:27–30 is called Peter's Confession. Jesus has directly asked his disciples, "Who do you say I am?" The same question Mark intends for the reader. Peter blurts out, "You are the Messiah!" We soon learn, however, that to be the messiah, the anointed king in the kingdom of God was quite different from being anointed king in the worldly kingdoms. Peter thought Jesus would now use his power and maybe even military might to impose his kingdom. Peter saw Jesus as messiah but had not seen clearly what that meant.

It is interesting that Mark gives us a foreshadowing of Peter's halfway insight. In the story that immediately precedes Peter's confession, Jesus cures a blind man at Bethsaida, but the blind man is only partially healed (Mark 8:22–26). He has sight but his sight is not clear—just as Peter's insight was unclear, incomplete. The second half of Mark's gospel—chapters 9 to 16—will help the reader "see" more clearly what it means for Jesus to be the messiah. It is obvious to us now that the first half of Mark corresponds to the first words we heard at Jesus' baptism—"You are my Son, the beloved." This quote from Psalm 2, a royal enthronement psalm, tells us that Jesus is the anointed king. The second half of Mark corresponds to the second phrase at Jesus' baptism, ". . . with you I am well pleased." Isaiah 42, a servant song, is the source of this quote and describes someone who suffers on behalf of others. We see that Jesus is a king who suffers. To be the king, the leader, in the kingdom of God Jesus would give himself away in service and love. Jesus' power was not coercion but example.

When Peter made his confession that Jesus was the messiah, Jesus sternly ordered him not to tell anyone about him (Mark 8:30). Why? Jesus knew Peter could only see half the picture. If Peter were to proclaim Jesus only as king, there would be no understanding of the servant role. Mark uses the remainder of the gospel to show Peter, the disciples, and the reader what it means to be a servant king. Jesus began this revealing by telling Peter that he, Jesus, will be rejected, suffer, and die (Mark 8:31). Peter, still not seeing clearly, rebukes Jesus (Mark 8:32). Jesus, in turn, rebukes Peter and gives a speech on discipleship. "If any want to become my followers, let them deny themselves, and take up their crosses and follow me" (Mark 8:34). Looking at the entire interaction with Peter, we see it has three parts: Jesus predicts his suffering, Peter and the disciples don't understand, and Jesus seeks to clarify. There are three such interactions in the second half of Mark—here at chapter 8, but also in chapters 9 and 10. These three "passion predictions," as they are called, are concluded with another healing of a blind person, Bartimaeus. "The blind man said to Jesus, 'My teacher, let me see again.' Jesus said to him, 'Go, your faith has made you well.' Immediately he regained his sight and followed him on the way" (Mark 10:51–52). Just as the cycle of passion predictions was preceded by the partial healing of a blind man, now, the conclusion of Jesus' attempts at clarification is the full healing of a blind man. Not only does Bartimaeus see who Jesus is, he follows Jesus on the "way." Bartimaeus's healing is more than physical but also spiritual. He sees clearly his life path. Early Christians must have taken this insight very seriously because they called themselves people of the way, the path. It is the same path of service and even suffering that the reader is invited to follow. The kingdom of God, life in its fullness, is "at hand" and is a journey with Jesus as teacher, guide, and inspiration.

Mark chapter 11 begins the final section of the gospel and describes the last week of Jesus' life. Here the king becomes the suffering servant and, in doing so, reveals to us the nature and the extent of God's love for us and identification with us. The section begins with Jesus' triumphal entry into Jerusalem. Jesus is received by the people as their messiah, their king; they were waving palm branches, like protest banners, as symbols of defiance to the Romans and national pride to the Jews. Immediately upon his entry, Jesus confronted the money changers in the temple complex, saying they had made it into a "den of robbers" (Mark 11:17). He struck a nerve and was subsequently confronted by one Jewish group after another—priests, Pharisees, Herodians, Sadducees, and scribes—until finally he was arrested at Passover. He was tried, condemned, sent to be crucified by Pontius Pilate, and abandoned by his disciples. Mark's description of Jesus' death is like a descent into darkness and despair with Mark only recording one statement of Jesus from the cross, "My God, my God, why have you forsaken me?" (Mark 15:34). At his death, however, a Roman centurion seemed to recognize just who Jesus was, "Truly this man was God's Son" (Mark 15:39). The question as to Jesus' identity has now been answered. Jesus is the king who suffers and dies. Jesus is God's Son who meets humanity in the darkness of death.

By telling the story of Jesus as he did, the gospel writer Mark emphasizes a theology of the cross—God meeting us and connecting with us in our despair, darkness and death. A theology of the cross might best be explained with a story. There was a young seminarian who was studying the theology of the cross when he suffered a near fatal illness. On Thanksgiving weekend, when he was finishing a paper on the theology of the cross, he experienced an ulcer which suddenly burst an artery in his stomach. A taxi brought him to the local trauma hospital where he was nauseous and weak from the bleeding. As a hospital gurney was readied, a nurse sat with this young man and held his head in her hands. He was vomiting. He was confused, terrified. He was going into a dark place . . . and he knew she was entering that place with him. She, too, was anxious and afraid. She felt some of what he felt. That connection, that identification brought a powerful sense of peace to the young man. He was not alone. From that experience he came to understand more personally the theology of the cross. Christ was like that nurse as he goes into the darkness that we all have or will experience. Prior to his bleeding ulcer—that theology of the cross moment— the seminarian always thought Jesus' death was about Jesus somehow paying for our sins as a sacrifice to God. We were bad and deserved punishment. Jesus was all good and took the penalty God required of us. A theology of the cross helped the seminarian consider another reason for Jesus' suffering and death. The cross was God's way of going with us into our suffering and death. God was not wrathful, demanding punishment for sin. God was gracious and loving, like that emergency room nurse. Sometimes people ask the question, "Where was God when some evil happened?" This question of theodicy has troubled humanity for centuries; a theology of the cross answers the question by saying, "God suffers too." God does not remain remote and insulated from the traumas of human existence, nor does God manipulate the world to bless some and curse others based on the fervency of prayer or the depth of faith. We have a theology of the cross God who meets us even at our darkest moments—and there is something wonderfully salvific about not being alone in this vast universe. God, the Higher Power, the Universal Presence—however you want to name the divine—cares about us enough to die with us.

Mark's theology of the cross is a powerful description of Jesus' death and it teaches us about the nature of God, but it tells us nothing of the resurrection, or heaven. The Gospel of Mark ends with the women—Mary, Mary Magdalene, and Salome—going to the tomb on the Sunday after the crucifixion to anoint Jesus' body. The stone was rolled away and an angel told the women that Jesus was not in the tomb, "He has been raised" (Mark 16:6). The women were then instructed to tell the story that Jesus was alive and they would see him again. The word "see" reminds the reader of all the people in the gospel who were blind to Jesus' identity and purpose. The women, in the final verse of the gospel, fled from the tomb in terror and amazement, and said "nothing to anyone" (Mark 16:17). (Please note many Bibles have two alternate endings to Mark's gospel which are resurrection accounts, neither of them, however, were originally written by Mark.) So why did Mark end his story of Jesus so abruptly? Why did Mark not describe a resurrection? It is possible that Mark leaves the gospel so unfinished because he wants the reader to continue the story. Although the text said the women said nothing to anyone, they must have told someone because we are still talking about Jesus today. Maybe Mark wants us to do the same, and not just tell the story that Jesus is alive but live the story of the kingdom of God? Jesus said the kingdom of God was at hand and proceeds to open our eyes to see that kingdom of compassion, justice, and peace. Like the blind man whose eyes were opened followed the path of Jesus, so it was with the women at the tomb and so it is with us. Maybe Mark neglects to mention heaven after we die because he wants us to follow the path of Jesus here and now? Maybe we are to be theologians of the cross who choose to join one another in the darkest of times? Maybe heaven for Mark is seeing Jesus in our neighbors and building an inclusive community where strangers are included? Maybe heaven for Mark is joining Jesus by going to the "other side" and reconciling with those cultures different from our own. Maybe the conclusion to the Gospel of Mark is still being written.

John's Theology of Glory

The Gospel of Mark emphasized Jesus' humanity, suffering, and death. The Gospel of John includes similar stories but added many more of Jesus' power and wisdom; Jesus is in control of every situation and conversation. John's gospel has sometimes been described with the metaphor of an eagle; it flies high philosophically and theologically, emphasizing a theology of glory, a view quite different from that of Mark's theology of the cross.

The overview of Mark's gospel includes Jesus doing ministry in the Galilee region, in the north of Israel, and taking one trip to Jerusalem, but John is structured in such a way that Jesus makes three trips to Jerusalem. The word "miracle" is never used, instead John uses the word "sign" to describe Jesus' acts of power. John includes these "signs" for their metaphoric power; everything in John seems to have a deeper meaning, where in Mark, all of Jesus' actions are direct and meant to be taken at face value.

The philosophical emphasis in John begins in chapter 1, verse 1, "In the beginning was the word, and the word was with God, and the word was God." Such a statement would have been understandable and appreciated by many of the sophisticated Greek-speaking Gentiles of the first century. John used the Greek word *logos*, which we translate as "word," because he knew it meant something specific to the Greek philosophical world. "Logos" was the underlying principle which oriented and gave meaning to the world and existence. Especially in relation to the philosophy of Plato, many Greeks believed that our material world was only a pale shadow of the real world—the world of ideals. John connects with these philosophers and they would agree that the divine "logos" was perfection itself, uncontaminated by the material world. The philosophers, however, were shocked when John in 1:14 boldly proclaims that the "word," the logos, became "flesh," that the spiritual became material. John continued in 1:14, "We have seen his glory . . . full of grace and truth." With this prologue enticing Jewish and Gentile readers, philosophers and lay people, John launches into his gospel by telling the story of Jesus as the "Logos" revealed in our midst.

Chapter 1 of John continues with Jesus being baptized by John the Baptist. There is no mystery as to Jesus' identity as there was in Mark; Jesus is call Logos, Son of God, Lamb of God, Rabbi, Messiah, and King of Israel, all in chapter 1.

Then, in chapters 2, 3, and 4, we read what appears to be three straightforward stories of Jesus' interactions with ordinary people. Each story stands alone and is carefully crafted to allow the insightful reader to grasp John's profound thoughts about Jesus and his mission.

Story one is the familiar Wedding at Cana story (John 2:1–12). Here Jesus attends a wedding feast and turns water into wine, which we think is an amazing miracle, or rather sign. We tend to view the story as some impossible physical transformation, but in the retelling by John, it is so much more. The water in the story was located at the front door of the house in six stone jars each holding twenty to thirty gallons—a significant amount of water . . . and of wine. The water at the door was used for a purification ritual. When good, observant Jews entered the home, they would ritually cleanse themselves with the water, washing away any contamination which may have afflicted them while out in the world. Jesus replaces this water of purification with wine of the highest quality. The symbolism of communion would have been obvious to the first-century reader. It was now, according to John, the blood of Christ which washed away that which contaminates and afflicts. The wedding feast itself became a symbol for the new Christian community. Like a wedding feast, there would be joy, peace, and abundance in Christ. The Christ community would be open, extravagant, inclusive; there would be food and drink for all. John's first story about Jesus—the word become flesh—is one of pure joy.

In chapter 3, John shares the story of Nicodemus, a leader of the Jews, coming by night to seek Jesus' wisdom. As in the Wedding at Cana story, Jesus is in control of the conversation, this time with one of the most important people in the country. Nicodemus is curious about Jesus and confesses that Jesus must be from God because of the signs (miracles) Jesus is able to perform, but Jesus moves past the focus on material signs of power and invites Nicodemus to "see" spiritually. In John 3:3, Jesus says, "No one can see the kingdom of God without being born again." The word "see" is quite symbolic as Nicodemus has not only come to Jesus by night, he has come in spiritual darkness. It is obvious that Nicodemus fails to "see" spiritually; he continues to see only the material world. "How can one be born after having grown old?" (John 3:4). Jesus attempts to open the eyes of Nicodemus. If we were to paraphrase Jesus it might go like this, "We can see with our material eyes and look always for some material miracle, but we can also look with our spiritual eyes and see the holiness of God's world all around us." The Greek philosophers who embraced the Platonic ideals would have understood this story; the real world is not simply the world of material, it is the world of the spirit. Jesus invites Nicodemus to be born into that world of spirit, but he is just too rooted in the world of shadows and material.

Finally, Jesus must spell it out for Nicodemus in one of the most familiar verses in the Bible—John 3:16, "For God so loved the world that he gave his only Son, so that everyone who believes in him may not perish but may have eternal life." John 3:16 has been a verse which has been used to separate those who adhere to a set of doctrines about Jesus and those who reject such doctrines. Some people, the one's who are true believers, will go to heaven and eternal life; while others, those who do not believe, will go the opposite direction. This interpretation of John 3:16 prevailed once Christianity became defined by doctrine, creeds, and church membership. We look at this verse through the lens of doctrine but if we look at John 3:16 in the context of John's gospel and the Nicodemus story, we interpret the verse with the lens of John's theology which gives us a different, more spiritual meaning. Two words are key—believe and eternal life. The word "believe" in the Greek of the Bible is much more than "thinking" something is true or false. Believe is not a doctrine word; it means to trust, to follow. Believe means to embrace a way of life and that way of life is suggested by the Greek word "eternal life." "Eternal life" is typically thought of in terms of quantity of life. We die and go to heaven to enjoy life forever in time. The Greek definition of the word is richer than mere quantity of time; it is also quality of life. Eternal life is life in its fullness. It is personal fulfillment and societal justice and peace. Jesus, throughout the book of John, and especially at John 3:16, is inviting the reader to "believe" or trust him to follow the path of "eternal life" both now and into eternity.

A third unique story (ch. 4) John shares with us takes place in Samaria—a non-Jewish area separating the Galilee region from the Judean area around Jerusalem. The Samaritans were not considered part of God's chosen people and when Jesus interacts with a woman at Jacob's well his disciples are shocked. Jesus sits by the well at noon, the heat of the day, when the Samaritan woman approaches with her water jug. She is surprised a Jewish man would even speak to her and confused when Jesus says he can give her living water. She is focused only on material, liquid water while Jesus, of course, is talking about something spiritual. We need physical water to sustain life, but life is more than material needs. Jesus says, "Those who drink of the water I will give them will never be thirsty. The water that I will give will become in them a spring of water gushing up to eternal life" (John 4:14). The woman, still confused, continues to be focused on her material needs but slowly she is coming to realize that Jesus is speaking to her about a full life—an "eternal life"—and such a life includes more than concerns about the day-to-day "stuff" of life. At the end of the story the woman is so excited about what she has learned from Jesus that she returns to the city to tell everyone about Jesus and the living, spiritual water. A small, almost obscure reference makes the point about our spiritual needs being just as important as our material needs. In John 4:28 the woman "left her water jar" and was so filled with the spiritual life that she became what Jesus predicted—a "spring of water gushing up to eternal life."

The three stories which open the Gospel of John clearly show us that Jesus is in charge and that he offers something deeply spiritual to the reader. John uses various metaphors for spiritual enlightenment—abundant wine symbolizes the joy of a wedding dance and life in the spirit; light is granted to a man living in darkness and coming to Jesus during the night time; and water of life for a woman who did not know she was spiritually thirsty. In the next few chapters, 6 through 10, Jesus continues to introduce "eternal or spiritual life" to many people and John continues his use of metaphor: healing to the sick and wounded, bread to those who are hungry, sight to the blind, and a good shepherd to those who are lost. In each example, John wants us to see beyond the material to the spiritual. Jesus offers the reader a holy, godly path—a path of spiritual enlightenment. That is why, toward the end of this section, Jesus can say, "The Father and I are one" (John 10:30). Christianity, of course, has taken such statements and built them into the doctrine that Jesus equals God and if you "think" this doctrine about Jesus is true then you are rewarded with heaven after you die. Putting the statement in the context of John's theology of glory, we realize Jesus is saying something more akin to:

"The Father and I are in tune with one another." Or, "Look to me and I will show you what your spiritual heart desires." Or, "Trust the path I show you and you will be fully alive." Jesus and his message, however, were fiercely resisted and that resistance fully forms in chapters 11 and 12.

Although John never uses the word "miracle" in his gospel, we often refer to the raising of Lazarus as one of Jesus' most miraculous actions. As with many of the other stories in John there is a surface meaning and something deeper. Jesus was on his way to Jerusalem for Passover when he's told of the death of his friend, Lazarus, the brother of Mary and Martha. Standing before the tomb, Jesus forcefully said, "Lazarus, come out!" (John 11:43). Lazarus, now alive, came out of the tomb and Jesus commanded his followers to unbind him from his graveclothes. On one level, this sign is a physical miracle, on a deeper level it points to Jesus' significance. There was a tradition in first-century Judaism that when the Messiah returned to usher in the Messianic Age of peace, justice, joy, and compassion, the dead would be raised to life. The raising of Lazarus was the final sign that Jesus was ushering in a new age—a new world which would threaten all the powers and privileges of the old world. The priests, the Pharisees, and the members of the Sanhedrin (the ruling council in Jerusalem) immediately knew their positions were threatened; they had accommodated themselves to the ways of injustice, inequality, and violence. Now they would have to rid themselves of this Jesus threat.

While the power people made their plans, John takes the reader to the upper room where Jesus and his disciples share a Seder (Passover) meal. John devotes five chapters to this upper room gathering (John 13–17) and in the "upper room discourses" Jesus shares what a godly, ideal community could be. It would be an enlightened community which would re-verse the top-down power and control of the world around them. Jesus mentions the word "glory" many times in these chapters and explains that "glory" comes with service and sacrifice. Jesus even washes his disciples' feet and commands them (Latin: maundatum) to wash one another's feet. In other words, in the godly community glory does not come from the ability to control but by the willingness to serve.

When Jesus tells his disciples that he is about to leave them, they are, of course, distraught and wonder aloud how they can continue. When Jesus says, "You know the way to the place where I am going" (John 14:4), the disciples are confused. Thomas asks, "Lord, we do not know where you are going. How can we know the way?" Jesus said to him, "I am the way, the truth, and the life. No one comes to the Father except through me" (John 14:5-7). We typically interpret this passage with our doctrinal glasses on. Believe Jesus is the Son of God who came to die for your sins and you can go to heaven after you die; if you don't believe in this doctrine you are con-demned. Such an interpretation ignores the word "way" in the passage and the emphasis on "eternal life"—the spiritually full life—which has been highlighted throughout the gospel. Jesus tells Thomas (and the reader) that he shows us a way—a path—to experience the bliss of eternal life both now and in the life to come. Jesus shows us the "glory" of this "eternal life" is meant for us as individuals and for society in general. There is no other path to individual and societal happiness than the upside-down values and priorities Jesus shows us. We have put so much emphasis on believing a doctrine about Jesus that we miss the full meaning of Jesus' message—"Embrace the way of life I show you and you will know eternal life, a spiritually full and happy life." This passage, which has been used too often to divide believer from nonbeliever, is more about those who follow the path of service and sacrifice Jesus modeled.

The final section of John's gospel narrates the trial, crucifixion, and resurrection of Jesus. Throughout John's description, Jesus continues to be the one in control. Where Mark describes Jesus' passive suffering and death, John's Jesus is active and managing events. Mark's theology of the cross meets John's theology of glory most profoundly in the story of Holy Week. Jesus and his disciples leave the upper room in John's chapter 18 and make their way to the garden of Gethsemane. There, Jesus is betrayed by Judas and confronted by soldiers and police who don't seem to know why they are there. It takes Jesus to ask the question, "Whom are you looking for?" (John 18:4). When the soldiers and police say, "Jesus of Nazareth," Jesus says, "I am he," and they step back and fall to the ground (John 18:4–6). In John's gospel, Jesus is completely in control of this and every situation; it is quite different from Mark's description of the arrest (Mark 14:43–50).

Jesus' trial is expanded in John and throughout Jesus continues to control events. Jesus shuttles between the high priest, Caiaphas, and the Roman procurator, Pontius Pilate. When he stands before Pilate, Pilate says he has the power of life or death over Jesus. Jesus is not intimidated and uses the opportunity to teach Pilate about the ways of the world and the ways of God. In the worldly kingdoms, power and control are exercised through violence and economic might—Pilate's kind of power. Jesus says that his kingdom is "not from the world" (John 18:36), meaning his godly kingdom is not like the worldly kingdoms; it operates with different rules and values. When Jesus says his kingdom is not of the world, he is not talking about heaven, he is describing a different vision for how people can live together in happiness and peace. Like Nicodemus in the night and the Samaritan woman at the well, Pilate is initially confused but slowly beginning to understand. Finally, Jesus says, "I came into the world to testify to the truth. Everyone who belongs to the truth hears my voice" (John 18:37). The "truth," of course, is the path, the way, Jesus shows his followers. It is a world with priorities flipped, where glory is giving oneself away washing feet. Pilate asks the question, "What is truth?" Is Pilate genuinely curious about this new world Jesus offers or is he cynical, caught on the career ladder of seeking ever greater dominance? Does Pilate know what Jesus is saying—that a full life (an eternal life) is found in loving relationships, reciprocal kindness, welcoming the stranger, and the joy of giving yourself to others? If indeed Pilate knew the kind of kingdom Jesus described, if he knew the "truth," he decides not to enter that world. Pilate had invested too much of himself in the world of hierarchical power. He may have known the difference between the two worlds—the two paths—but he could not step onto the Jesus path. He believed he would give up too much—his position, security, and material wealth. Pilate gave in to the political pressure placed on him by the mob and so ordered Jesus crucified. His one last bit of honesty was to put a sign on the cross—Jesus of Nazareth, King of the Jews.

Throughout the trial and crucifixion in John's gospel, Jesus is serene, dignified, and in control. In Mark, Jesus is victimized and only speaks once from the cross, "My God, my God, why have you forsaken me?" (Mark 15:34). John does not include that dark statement but rather records Jesus' concern for his mother, giving instructions for her care. He also says, "I thirst" (John 19:28), and finally, "It is finished" (John 19:30). "It is finished," can also be rendered, "It is accomplished." Or, "It is completed." Or, "I have done it." The cross is a glorious accomplishment in John, in Mark the cross is a descent into darkness.

Where Mark records no resurrection appearance, John shares several. On the first day of the week, he appeared to Mary Magdalene and asked her the same question he asked the soldiers and the police in the garden of Gethsemane, "Whom are you looking for?" Mary does not recognize Jesus until he calls her by name and when she falls at his feet, Jesus cryptically remarks, "Do not hold onto me!" (John 20:17). Did he mean that she must now walk her own spiritual path? In the evening of that first resurrection day, Jesus appeared to the disciples in a locked room and said, "Peace be with you. Receive the Holy Spirit" (John 20:19–23). He assures them they would not be alone as they followed him on the way of the spirit. Then, a week later, Jesus appeared again, this time to the disciples and to Thomas, who was absent at earlier appearances. Jesus shows Thomas the wounds on his hands and side and Thomas falls on his knees and proclaims, "My Lord and my God." The passage should be titled "Believing Thomas" rather than the more familiar "Doubting Thomas." The chapter ends with John making an invitation to the reader, "Now Jesus did many other signs . . . but these are written so that you may come to believe [i.e., trust, follow] that Jesus is the messiah, the Son of God and that through believing [trusting, following] you may have life [spiritual life] in his name" (John 20:30, 31).

John's theology of glory tells the story of Jesus from a perspective quite different from Mark's theology of the cross. In the theology of glory, Jesus moves through the sorrows and rejection of the world with dignity, grace, and strength. In the theology of the cross, Jesus enters the pain and darkness, dying with us. John's theology of glory celebrates a Jesus who rises above the material world and shows us a path to spiritual fulfillment. Which perspective, Mark's or John's, is correct? Each has its points to make about Jesus and the two views need not be reconciled. They can stand independently, giving us insight from their different angles on the story. Maybe we have four different gospels for the very reason that Jesus Christ must be viewed from more than one perspective. Matthew and Luke, the remaining two gospels, add their own emphases which, like Mark versus John, seem to almost contradict each other. Matthew emphasizes the teaching of Jesus and a new chosen people, while Luke will emphasize the compassionate, inclusive Jesus and a new human race.

Discussion Questions

1. What was your reaction to learning that Mark's gospel ends without a resurrection account?

2. The dominant atonement theory in history has been Jesus as a sacrifice for our sins. What do you think of an atonement theory which de-emphasizes sacrifice and emphasizes Jesus joining humanity in suffering and death as an act of complete and gracious love on God's part?

3. Have you ever had someone join you in suffering? Have you ever gone into the pain of someone else? Describe the healing that happens even if the suffering continues.

4. Where Mark emphasizes Jesus' suffering and death, John celebrates Jesus' triumph over the grave. John's theology of glory finds powerful expression in the church's extravagant and beautiful Easter celebrations. Describe a glorious experience of Christ alive in your life. Was it a public experience? A private experience?

5. How can the theology of the cross and the theology of glory find balance in your life and the life of the church?

—— *Chapter Six* ——

Matthew's New Chosen People vs. Luke's New Human Society

THE GOSPEL OF MARK told the Jesus story through the prism of a theology of the cross while John told it through a theology of glory. Reading both stories helps us get a more complete picture of who Jesus was and is for many Christians today. Matthew and Luke might also be compared with each other. Matthew's audience must be primarily Jewish with his many references to the Old Testament (Torah) and his implication that Jesus is like a new Moses inaugurating a new chosen people. Just as Moses brought the torah to bind the chosen people Israel together, now Jesus teaches a new torah to bind what he calls the kingdom of heaven together. Luke's audience is much wider than Matthew's. He speaks to the entire Roman world with a message of reversal. God lifts up the lowly, the oppressed, and the poor and brings low those who are rich and powerful. Where Matthew seems to emphasize Jesus creating and teaching a new chosen people, Luke proclaims a new human society. As with the Mark/John comparison, Matthew/Luke appear quite different from each other, even contradictory, but, as we allow the differences to stand, we are blessed to see Jesus from various perspectives.

The Gospel of Matthew, as all the gospels, is carefully crafted and so it is important to look at an overview of the gospel to understand Matthew's purpose. Mark, as you remember, was written as a mystery story about Jesus' identity. The first eight chapters give us a series of hints which crescendo with Peter's confession that Jesus is the Christ, the Messiah. Mark then takes us back down from the crescendo showing us that the Christ, the Messiah, suffers and dies to fully identify with humanity. Matthew must have been familiar with Mark's gospel because he copies many of Mark's verses word for word. He also uses the broad outline of Mark—Jesus does ministry in the Galilee region, makes one trip to Jerusalem, and is there crucified. Matthew takes that broad outline of sixteen chapters and expands the story with five new sections primarily of Jesus' teaching giving a total of twenty chapters. By adding five new teaching sections, Jewish readers of Matthew would have associated the gospel with the Pentateuch—the first five books of the Bible—the books of Moses. Matthew's intention is to reach a Jewish audience because he frames the story in such a way that Jesus is now to be considered a new Moses and the promised Messiah of Old Testament prophecy.

In addition to the teaching sections, Matthew adds an infancy narrative to the story line he received from Mark. He does so for an interesting purpose—to show Jesus' connection with the origins of the Jewish people. With a long genealogy, Matthew begins by showing Jesus is connected to King David and even further back to Abraham and Sarah. The infancy narrative has only one sentence describing Jesus' actual birth (Matt 1:25). An entire chapter is then devoted to Jesus and his parents fleeing the wrath of King Herod and going down as refugees to Egypt, then just as the

Hebrew people and Moses came out of Egypt, so did Jesus and his parents. Moses and the Hebrew people go through a water crossing—the Red Sea. Jesus returns from Egypt in Matthew chapter 2, but already in chapter 3 he is an adult and is baptized in the River Jordan. Like the Hebrew slaves, baptism is Jesus' "water crossing." Moses and the Hebrew people follow the Red Sea crossing with forty years in the wilderness. Jesus follows his water baptism with forty days in the wilderness. By the time we reach chapter 5 of Matthew, the comparison to Moses is obvious; so, when we read that Jesus "saw the crowds and went up the mountain" (Matt 5:1), we are thinking Jesus is going to give a new set of Ten Commandments to match Moses on Mount Sinai. Instead of a new set of commandments, which are often called the torah, Jesus gives us the Beatitudes. The word "torah" means a "teaching"; now Jesus gives us a new teaching which will bind the new chosen people together.

Matthew 5:3-11 has nine "beatitudes"—Latin for "blessed"—and together they form the first major teaching section in Matthew with the first beatitude setting the tone for the remaining eight, "Blessed are the poor in spirit for theirs is the kingdom of heaven" (Matt 5:3). Matthew does not describe Jesus giving us a new set of commandments but rather a description of God's care and concern for those at the bottom of society—the wounded, persecuted, reviled, meek, grieving, compassionate, and innocent people who are so rarely appreciated or even noticed. Matthew continues in the next chapters to share Jesus' words about the interpretation of the law and the nature of the kingdom of heaven. Here Jesus says to his listeners they are the "salt of the earth" (Matt 5:13); they are the ones that preserve and form the vision of a compassionate, loving society. Here

Jesus says he has not come to abolish the law but to fulfill it (Matt 5:17). The original torah was not meant to simply be a set of rules but the way a just society can be structured. Jesus will change people's hearts and minds, inspiring them to fulfill the intent of the law; they will desire to be God's people and will not need rules to make them so. Here Jesus says, "Anyone who strikes you on the right cheek, turn the other also" (Matt 5:39) and "love your enemies and pray for those who persecute you" (Matt 5:44). Here Jesus shares the Golden Rule, "Do onto others as you would have them do onto you" (Matt 7:12). These are not a new set of commandments, rather they are descriptions of a godly people, the kingdom of heaven. It is difficult for us to move beyond our fixation on rules; if we follow the rule—commandment—we think we have earned the right to be chosen. Jesus is teaching his followers here that an ethical, moral community begins with people whose very hearts and minds are changed. It is like the student who was studying the Beatitudes and said to the professor, "I think I understand. Mother Teresa did all the loving things Jesus teaches but not because they were rules to follow. It is who she has become. Her heart is changed. She has genuine compassion and love for the world around her and her actions follow." This young man came to appreciate Matthew's description of Jesus' teaching in chapters 5 to 7 as one of the most sublime and inspirational recordings in all world literature. Matthew then ends this teaching section as he does all the others, with the words "Jesus finished these sayings" (Matt 7:29).

In the next two chapters (8 and 9) Matthew continues the narrative about what Jesus is doing and then, in chapter 10, Jesus is again teaching. In the second teaching section, Jesus explains that the kingdom of heaven—where a new chosen people are living out the Beatitudes—can be threatening to many and many will reject it. The narrative returns in chapters 11 and 12; and then in teaching section 3, chapter 13, Jesus teaches using short pithy parables, many beginning with, "The kingdom is heaven is like . . ." good seed falling on fertile soil, a mustard seed that is small but grows to be huge, yeast which is leavening for the whole loaf (the whole society), a treasure hidden in a field, and a pearl of great price. Chapter 18 is the fourth teaching section and it, again, describes life in the kingdom of heaven. In the fifth and final teaching section (Matt 24, 25) Jesus challenges his followers to be attentive, aware and active in waiting for and promoting the kingdom of heaven. Here we read the parable of the ten bridesmaids who trim their lamps and are ready when the bridegroom arrives. Here is the parable of the talents where we learn talents are to be used not hoarded. The kingdom of heaven is in our midst and we work to create it but we also wait for its fullness yet to come.

In the fifth and final teaching section Matthew writes, "All nations will be gathered before him and he will separate people one from another as a shepherd separates the sheep from the goats" (Matt 25:32). The sheep inherit the "kingdom prepared for you from the foundations of the world" (Matt 25:34). We assume "inheriting the kingdom" means going to heaven after we die but is that what Jesus means? Throughout the Gospel of Matthew, Jesus has been teaching about the kingdom of heaven and he continually references life in this world. The kingdom of heaven is not only life after death; the kingdom of heaven is God's intention for human beings to live in harmony now. The entire Bible—Old and New Testaments—speaks of God creating a community of kindness, compassion, and justice. Moses and the Ten

Commandments were intended to create such a society. The prophets of old called the people back to such a kingdom. Now Jesus in Matthew describes the nature of the "kingdom of heaven." The kingdom of heaven is concerned about the lonely and forgotten, the oppressed and poor. The kingdom of heaven is about living spiritually not just for material well-being. The kingdom of heaven is not personal salvation, it is salvation for society. We identify with this vision of how the world should be. In fact, most people on earth—religious and secular—yearn for just such a society.

With an understanding of the biblical emphasis that salvation is not just for individuals but for society, we look again at Matthew 25. Jesus has just described how the sheep and goats are separated. The sheep inherit the kingdom and the goats are sent away. We might think the sheep represent good, orthodox Christians and the goats, atheist unbelievers—some are saved and some are lost. Jesus, however, does not describe such a doctrinal criterion. Instead, Jesus says about the "sheep," ". . . for I was hungry and you gave me food, I was thirsty and you gave me something to drink, I was a stranger and you welcomed me, I was naked and you gave me clothing, I was sick and you took care of me, I was in prison and you visited me" (Matt 25:35–36). Jesus' description of those who treat others with such respect and kindness matches perfectly with his many descriptions of the kingdom of heaven earlier in the gospel. Are those who show such compassionate behavior already experiencing the kingdom of heaven? The moments where such kindness exists may be rare, as tiny as a mustard seed, but such is the kingdom of heaven present now. Are those who refuse to reach out to others already beginning to experience the opposite of the kingdom of heaven?

In the final verse of chapter 25, Jesus says, "And these will go away into eternal punishment, but the righteous into eternal life." Matthew shares Jesus' words about judgment in the future, but that judgment is not based on orthodox thinking, nor church membership, nor some religious experience. As Matthew completes his record of Jesus' teaching, we have seen that "kingdom of heaven," not doctrine, has been the major criterion determining who are sheep and who are goats. It is important to note that Jesus does not teach doctrine, yet Christianity, in all its denominations and manifestations, has relied almost exclusively on doctrinal statements to define who is part of God's kingdom and who is not. Christian doctrine has perpetuated a zero-sum thinking in the church and even in Western civilization by emphasizing those who are in and those who are out, those who are saved and those lost, those who are winners and those who are losers. It is not what Jesus intended. Jesus defines the kingdom ethically, morally, and relationally. His is not an either/or definition. Jesus does not give rules to obey or doctrines to follow, but instead describes human beings living to their highest ideals in a society of compassion. Sometimes we live fully into these ideals and sometimes we do not. We are at times sheep and, at times, goats. There are moments, tiny mustard seed moments, when we live and experience the kingdom, and other moments when we are selfish, angry, and violent. Jesus teaches us to live into the kingdom of heaven and, even though we will fail as often as succeed, Jesus assures us the kingdom of heaven is our future and the future of creation. With ultimate optimism Jesus notices the seeds of goodness in ourselves and in our world and predicts that what seems like the tiniest of seeds will grow to become the mightiest of trees providing shelter for all God's creatures—the kingdom of heaven.

Matthew now takes us to the end of his gospel. He has continued to follow the broad outline of Mark, adding in the teaching sections, but now he changes the ending. Matthew takes Mark's abrupt ending—where the women "flee the tomb and say nothing to anyone for they were afraid"—and adds they were "filled with great joy" (Matt 28:8). Matthew's Jesus then said to the women, "Do not be afraid" (Matt 28:10). It is interesting that Jesus says, "Do not be afraid," rather than, "Do not doubt." We often think the opposite of faith is doubt primarily because we have defined faith as adherence to certain doctrines about Jesus. Here Jesus teaches the opposite of faith is fear. We are often fearful to risk living fully into the kingdom of heaven—the kingdom of kindness, compassion, sacrifice, and justice—because we might lose our earthly security. We would rather turn our religion into a set of doctrines to which we give our intellectual assent and which require little sacrifice. Believing doctrine seems much safer than taking the risk to live compassionately.

At the very end of his gospel, Matthew reports Jesus' final teaching to his disciples, "Go therefore, and make disciples [followers] of all nations, baptizing them in the name of the Father, and of the Son, and of the Holy Spirit, teaching them to observe all that I have commanded you, and lo, I am with you always, to the close of the age" (Matt 28:19–20). Matthew has recorded Jesus' teaching about the kingdom of heaven. It is now the turn of the disciples to become teachers, but not simply teachers of doctrine or theological insight, they teach so that followers will "observe"—put into practice what has been taught.

Luke's New Human Society

The Gospel of Matthew used many references to the Old Testament and was, presumably, intended for a Jewish audience. The Gospel of Luke's audience is much broader—the entire Roman Empire. We get a hint of the broader perspective in chapter 1 where we read the genealogy of Jesus. Where Matthew traces Jesus' ancestry back to Abraham and Sarah—the parents of the Jewish people—Luke traces Jesus' line back to Adam and Eve—the parents of humanity. In Luke's gospel version, Jesus would touch all humanity with a message similar to the other gospels, that of Jesus inaugurating a just and compassionate world. The story of Jesus in Luke proclaims a great reversal for human society. The lowly will be lifted up and the mighty, brought low. Matthew proclaimed a new chosen people, while Luke proclaims a new human race. Reading Luke with this universal lens, we can unlock the reasons Luke told the Jesus story the way he did.

Luke, like Matthew, must have had a copy of Mark's gospel available to him because he uses Mark's broad outline and many of Mark's words. Jesus is raised in the Galilee region and does a majority of his ministry there. He takes one major trip to Jerusalem, where he is arrested, crucified, and raised from the dead. Luke, however, again like Matthew, adds to the Markan outline. Matthew added five major teaching sections; Luke adds an entire new book—the book of Acts. Luke's gospel is written in two parts. Luke itself tells the story of Jesus' life while Acts records the spread of the gospel from Jerusalem to the city of Rome. The gospel would touch the center of the empire. In addition to an entire additional book, Luke also adds a major section to his gospel. Luke had a theological purpose to emphasize and he does so throughout the book but especially in what is called the "travel document." Where Mark and Matthew have a very brief account of Jesus traveling from Galilee to Jerusalem, Luke expands this trip to ten chapters (Luke 9–19)! In these chapters, as he does throughout the book, Luke proclaims a gospel of great reversal—the powerless are lifted up even above imperial Rome.

Luke begins his gospel by greatly expanding the story of Jesus' birth. Mark has no infancy narrative, Matthew has only a verse, but Luke has two chapters. We are familiar with Luke chapter 2—the traditional birth of Jesus we read each Christmas. It is preceded by angelic proclamations to Zechariah and Elizabeth, parents of John the Baptist, and additional proclamations to Mary, Jesus' mother. Upon learning she would bear the Christ child, Mary is inspired by the words of Hannah from the book of 1 Samuel and shares a hymn of praise we call the Magnificat (Luke 1:46–55). One sentence especially states the great reversal theme, "He has brought down the powerful from their thrones, and lifted up the lowly; he has filled the hungry with good things, and sent the rich away empty" (Luke 1:52–53).

The beautiful account of Jesus' birth in Luke chapter 2 has become so familiar and sentimental that it is easy to miss its radical nature and how it is also an example of Luke's great reversal emphasis. The chapter begins with a reference to Emperor Augustus, who sat atop the largest, most powerful empire the world had ever seen. Augustus had ordered a census for tax purposes and off Mary and Joseph went, to Bethlehem, the hometown of Joseph. Mary was "expecting a child" (Luke 2:5), and when she was ready to deliver, there was no room for them in the inn. Mary gave birth to Jesus in the back of a barn and he was placed in a feeding trough for animals. Jesus was born into utter poverty and the contrast to Emperor Augustus could not be greater.

The first to hear of the birth of Jesus were the shepherds "keeping watch over their flocks by night" (Luke 2:8). We imagine the sentimental scene, influenced by all the Sunday School programs featuring children wearing bathrobes as modern-day shepherds. The first-century shepherds, however, were people living on the fringe of society. They had a dirty job and they were considered ritually unclean by the temple officials. To these outcast shepherds the angel of the Lord said, "To you is born this day in the city of David a Savior, who is the Messiah, the Lord" (Luke 2:11). The shepherds may have wondered especially at the word "savior." Certainly anyone reading the Gospel of Luke would have know that the "savior" was used to describe Emperor Augustus. After all, Augustus, whose name was Octavian, had defeated Antony and Cleopatra and patched the Roman Empire back together after years of civil war. Augustus had saved the Roman world from anarchy and was now initiating a time of peace across the Mediterranean that has come to be know as the Pax Romana. What did it mean that a baby born into poverty is also called "savior"? Luke here proclaims a different kind of savior for a different kind of empire.

In the next chapter Luke gives a strong hint at the nature of the Jesus "empire" by adding an additional sentence to John the Baptist's speech announcing the coming Messiah. Like Matthew, Luke begins John's quote of Isaiah 40:3–5, "The voice of one crying in the wilderness: 'Prepare the way of the Lord, make his paths straight.'" Luke, but not Matthew, continues, "Every valley shall be filled, and every mountain and hill shall be made low, and the crooked shall be made straight, and the rough ways made smooth; *and all flesh shall see the salvation of God.*" Luke, by including "all flesh" to the salvation of God, emphasizes Jesus' universal and "empire-sized" ministry. Luke is not just proclaiming a new chosen people but a new human race.

In Luke chapter 4, the universal and great reversal themes continue when Jesus returns to his hometown of Nazareth to teach in the synagogue. He takes the scroll of Isaiah and reads, "The spirit of the Lord is upon me, because he has anointed me to bring good news to the poor. He has sent me to bring good news to the poor. He has sent me to proclaim release to the captives and recovery of sight to the blind, to let the oppressed go free, and to proclaim the year of the Lord's favor" (Luke 4:18–19). The "year of the Lord's favor" was the year of Jubilee described in Leviticus 25:8–12, and was to be celebrated every fiftieth year (a sabbatical of sabbatical of years). In that year all debts would be forgiven and all people would start over with equal ownership of the land. It was a radical redistribution of wealth and was never fully practiced in ancient Israel. (As an aside, it is interesting that some Christians will pull out of the Old Testament rather obscure passages which match a certain cultural or political belief, but never do we hear people calling for a full Jubilee year.) Jubilee must have been threatening to the people of Nazareth because when Jesus states he has come to inaugurate such a Jubilee, he is driven out of his hometown. Few people want the great reversal of fortunes Jubilee promises.

Luke continues to view Jesus with a different lens from Matthew when we get to the Beatitudes. In Matthew Jesus goes up the mountain like a new Moses to deliver the Beatitudes, but in Luke Jesus does so by "standing on a level place" (Luke 6:17). He then quotes Jesus differently from Matthew. Matthew chapter 5 has, "Blessed are the poor in spirit," and Luke has, "Blessed are the poor." Luke puts an emphasis on the economically destitute, Matthew on the spiritually destitute. Luke has, "Blessed are you who are hungry," and Matthew has, "Blessed are those who hunger and thirst for righteousness" (Matt 5:6). Luke adds a series of "woes" which Matthew does not include. "Woe to the rich . . . woe to those who are full now," etc. (Luke 6:24). In Luke the emphasis is on the great reversal—the lowly are elevated and the mighty are brought low.

The large travel document, unique to Luke, also highlights Luke's themes of the universal dimensions of Jesus' ministry and that of the great reversal. Beginning in Luke 9:51 the travel document continues through Luke 19:27, and throughout we hear parables which emphasize Luke's theological priorities. The parable of the Good Samaritan is a prime example and is found only in Luke. A lawyer questions of Jesus, "What must I do to inherit eternal life?" (Luke 10:25). Jesus responds, "What is written in the law?" The lawyer answers well, "You shall love the Lord your God with all your heart, and with all your strength, and with all your mind; and your neighbor as yourself." The parable of the Good Samaritan is told to answer the lawyer's next question, "Just who is my neighbor?" In other words, "Just who is it I must show love?" In the parable Jesus describes a man going to Jericho who is attacked by robbers and left near death on the side of the road. A priest and then a Levite, good religious Jews, pass by on the other side of the road and ignore the wounded man, but a Samaritan, someone despised as a foreigner, stopped to help the man. Jesus makes a double point here—we are called to help the wounded and our neighbors are not only people we know, people of our group, but the foreigner and stranger. We are to love the man who was wounded, also the foreigner, the other, the enemy. Jesus' "empire of God" would not be tribal in nature, it would be inclusive, diverse, and cosmopolitan.

Throughout the ten chapters of Luke's travel document, Jesus continually shares parables and teaches his disciples that wealth, position, and power in this age—the kingdom/ empire of Augustus—are to contrast with the values, priorities, and inclusiveness of the kingdom/empire of God. Here we have the parables of the great dinner where the host invites many but many refuse, so the banquet is opened to the "poor, the blind, and the lame" (Luke 14:21). We also read the parable of the lost sheep where the shepherd leaves the ninety-nine and searches until the one lost sheep is found (Luke 15:1–7). We read the parables of the Lost Coin, the Prodigal Son, and the Rich Man and Lazarus. Luke tells us of the cleansing of the ten lepers where the only one who returns to thank and praise Jesus is an outsider—a Samaritan. There is the arrogant Pharisee and the humble tax collector, the regularly ignored children who Jesus insists must come to him, the rich ruler who cannot give all he has to the poor, and Zacchaeus, a wee little man, despised by the crowds but loved by Jesus. All these stories and more are shared by Luke, which bolster his theological points of universal inclusiveness and great reversal. In the empire of Jesus, the savior, it would be the outsiders, the poor, the lost, and the neglected ones who would be first and the privileged and rich ones in the empire of Augustus who would be last.

The travel document ends at Luke 19:27 and Luke picks up the narrative of Jesus' final week in Jerusalem. Luke uses Mark's Holy Week sequence of events but here and there makes additions and deletions. One example is Luke's record of what Jesus speaks from the cross. In chapter 23, verse 34,

Jesus says, "Father, forgive them; for they do not know what they are doing." Throughout the gospel, Jesus has offered forgiveness and welcomed to the empire of God people who were outsiders, wounded, forgotten, or sinners. Here he forgives even the soldiers ordered to nail him to the cross. Later, Jesus speaks to the one criminal who repented and welcomes him to God's empire, "Truly, I tell you, today you will be with me in paradise" (Luke 23:43). The final word from the cross in Luke is not recorded in Mark or Matthew. They both say simply that Jesus breathed his last and gave up his spirit. John has Jesus say, "It is finished [accomplished]" (John 19:30). Luke, however, has, "Father into your hands I commend my spirit." It is a confident passing from one kingdom to another. Jesus has promoted the kingdom/empire of God on earth in this life and now he will know its fullness in the life to come. Luke also changes the words coming from the mouth of the centurion at Jesus' death. Instead of "Surely, this was the Son of God," Luke records, "Certainly this man was innocent" (Luke 23:47). An additional meaning of the word "innocent" is "righteous," which matches well with Luke's theology. Jesus was in right relationship with God and the world. He lived compassion, forgiveness, inclusivity, and love; all signs of righteousness in the empire of God. Maybe, just maybe, the Roman soldier became aware of his own place in the domineering, top-down, unrighteous empire of Rome.

Following Jesus' crucifixion Luke follows Matthew's lead by describing other resurrection appearances, with one account being unique to Luke. On the day of resurrection two disciples are walking to the town of Emmaus. A stranger joins the two but the disciples do not recognize it is Jesus until that evening when they share a meal. Jesus takes the bread, blesses and breaks it. He gives it to them and their "eyes were opened, and they recognized him" (Luke 24:30–31). Jesus then vanishes from their sight. It is a cryptic story which at a minimum reminds us of Jesus' presence in the bread and wine of communion. Later that same evening the two disciples return to Jerusalem and share with the other disciples their experience meeting Jesus. Suddenly, Jesus stands in their midst and says, "Peace be with you" (Luke 24:36) and asks for something to eat and proceeds to summarize his purpose on earth—that "repentance and forgiveness of sins be proclaimed in God's name to *all the nations*" (Luke 24:47). Luke continues his theological emphasis of universality by recognizing Jesus' mission to all the nations, not just a chosen few. The kingdom/empire of God would challenge the kingdom/empire of the powerful few in a great and holy reversal.

Here Luke ends the first of his two-part gospel, with the second half being the book of Acts. The Acts of the Apostles is the story of the gospel of God's kingdom/empire being proclaimed to all the nations. Acts begins in Jerusalem and then follows the message, proclaimed by the disciples, Paul, and others, to the "ends of the earth," symbolized by the city of Rome. All roads led to Rome and all roads to the nations led from Rome. Just as the empire of Augustus branched out to dominate all the Mediterranean world, now a new empire would follow those same roads to inaugurate an empire of compassion, forgiveness, and justice.

The Gospels of Matthew and Luke tell the story of Jesus from different perspectives and with their own theological agendas. Matthew presents Jesus as a new Moses, reinterpreting the law for a new chosen people. The new chosen people would be bound together with an ethic of love and compassion—the fulfillment of God's intention revealed in the Old

83

Testament. Luke presents Jesus as a new Augustus, a new kind of savior, a different form of emperor. Augustus's empire and all worldly empires are based on violence, coercion, and economic clout, where only a few are elevated above the many. The empire Jesus creates is based on God's grace and compassion, where forgiveness, inclusivity, and justice prevail. It is the great reversal of the Roman Empire and all worldly empires to follow. Luke and Matthew present different perspectives on the Jesus story. Which is correct? Which is true? They both are, and both are valuable for us to get the best picture of who Jesus is for us and for the world.

Discussion Questions

1. Matthew wrote his gospel of Jesus emphasizing Christ as the fulfillment of many Old Testament prophecies. Jesus was a new kind of Moses giving a new torah or teaching, e.g., the Beatitudes in chapter 5. How is learning an important part of your faith life?

2. We have traditionally defined Christianity and its many denominations with sets of often competing doctrines. Doctrines are really teachings about the faith. How would you define what it means to be a Christian?

3. Teaching and learning can also extend to the devotional life. The devotional life is personal, prayerful, and reflective. Describe how, when, and where you turn inward to experience God's presence.

4. Reflection in faith life can be symbolized by one end of an infinity figure—the sideways eight—while the other side could represent our actions in the world. Luke especially celebrates a faith in action—the Good Samaritan story is a perfect example. Give example of faith in action.

5. How does your life find a faith balance between reflection and action? How might you find such a balance?

—— *Chapter Seven* ——

Paul vs. James

THE FOUR GOSPELS COMPOSE only a part of the New Testament; there are twenty-three other New Testament books with various authors who sometimes contradict each other. One obvious example would be the Apostle Paul and James, the brother of Jesus, both of whom write about faith and works. Paul writes about faith as being sufficient for salvation (e.g., Rom 3:26) while James writes that "faith without works is dead" (Jas 2:26). These two statements appear to contradict each other but again, it can be a blessing to read the two and allow the tension to give us a balanced appreciation of scripture.

The Apostle Paul is credited with writing as many as nine of the New Testament books, all of them letters. Paul, whose Jewish name was Saul, grew up in a city called Tarsus, located in a province of the Roman Empire which is now part of modern Turkey. He was an observant Jew in the Pharisaic tradition and a citizen of the empire, which allowed him to straddle the two worlds of Gentile Rome and Jewish Jerusalem. Paul became a critical interpreter of the Jewish Christian movement for an empire-wide Gentile audience. Paul, however, was not always a supporter of the Jesus movement. The book of Acts portrays Saul/Paul as a persecutor of the Christians, and a feared one at that. While on his way to the city of Damascus, Saul, who was to become commonly known as Paul, had a dramatic religious experience. A light shined so brilliantly around him that it threw him from his horse. Blinded, Paul heard a voice; it was Jesus, who said, "Saul, Saul why do you persecute me?" (Acts 9:4). For three days Paul was blind, in the dark like his own tomb of uncertainty, until a man named Ananias healed Paul and he was filled with the Holy Spirit. From that moment Paul became a supporter and advocate for the Christian movement and through his missionary endeavors, many letters, and sophisticated theology, opened the Judaic Christian movement to an empire-wide Gentile audience.

James, who was the brother of Jesus, became the leader of the Christian church in Jerusalem. We do not know as much about James as we do Paul, but it is obvious from the one letter we do have that he was heavily influenced by Jewish tradition as it related to developing Christian theology. As Christianity spread throughout the Mediterranean world, Paul's theology became more influential than that of James and a central pillar of Paul's theology was his understanding of faith and works, and how they related to salvation. Paul sets forth a radical understanding of faith alone as adequate for salvation and described his thinking in many letters including the one to the people of Galatia. Paul visited Galatia, a Roman province in central Asia minor (present Turkey), not far from his hometown of Tarsus, and had established new church communities there. After leaving the area, Paul was informed that other missionaries were visiting Galatia and were contradicting Paul's theological message. These later missionaries, called Judaizers, preached that a person must follow the Jewish laws and show good works to be saved. Paul's letter, the book of Galatians, strongly responded to the Judaizers and articulated a theology which was and is inspiring and controversial.

In Galatians 2:16, 17, Paul writes, "Yet we know that a person is *justified* not by works of the law but through *faith in Jesus Christ*, and not by doing works of the law, because no one will be justified by works of the law." These verses seem less than radical to us, partly because many of us are familiar with the Protestant phrase, proclaimed by Martin Luther, that we are "justified by grace through faith," but even Lutherans typically fail to appreciate the radicality of what originally was Paul's theological revolution. We talk about faith alone for salvation, but we easily turn faith into a kind of work. Yes, we are justified by God's grace through faith, so we must try hard to have faith. If a person does not have enough faith, try harder, work at it. Faith becomes something to be accomplished by the individual believer. Paul would have opposed such thinking with as much vigor as he opposed the Judaizers.

To fully appreciate the radical nature of Paul's preaching to the Galatians, we must do a lesson in grammar. In the passage from Galatians quoted above, some words have been italicized because they are key to understanding Paul's theology and why it was/is so difficult to accept. First, the word "justified" is important because it is a term from the legal world which reinstates to society someone who has committed a crime. When a criminal has broken the norms of society and, in a sense, has left society, it is the purpose of the justice system to provide a pathway for the person to return to good standing. To be justified with God is to be brought back into good standing with God and into the ways of God. Early Christians understood their justification with God and described themselves as people of "the way" rather than by people of a certain doctrine or creed. Justification was thought of as returning to the ways of God and, additionally, to the community of God's people—the kingdom of God.

To be justified in the legal system sometimes means a penalty, like paying a fine, or serving incarceration time. Sometimes it means taking classes or being assigned some form of personal growth like court-ordered attendance at AA meetings. The question Paul is dealing with in Galatians is just how do we reenter the pathway and community of God; how do we enter the good and righteous life God intends for us? Paul says it happens through the other italicized passage above—"faith in Jesus Christ." This is where our grammar lesson becomes critical to understanding Paul's revolutionary theology. The little preposition "in" and how we translate it, is the key to the whole passage and to Paul's theology. The preposition is in the genitive case which means it implies ownership. In this case we understand the word "in" as objective genitive, that is, Jesus is the direct object of the faith. We are the ones who have the faith and direct it toward Jesus. The genitive case can also be understood as subjective genitive which would mean the translation would not be "faith in Jesus" but "faith of Jesus." In subjective genitive, Jesus is the subject, and faith the object. It is the faith that Jesus has that saves us not the faith we have. Subjective versus objective genitive can be explained with the phrase "love of mother." The meaning is ambiguous; it could mean our love for our mother (objective genitive) or a mother's love for us (subjective genitive). The two possible meanings of the genitive in English match the two possible meanings in the Greek of the New Testament leaving us with a decision about which genitive Paul intended. Is it our faith that saves? Or Jesus' faith?

All this talk about subjective and objective genitive may seem obscure but it makes a significant difference for theology. Does Paul mean we are saved by our faith in Jesus (objective genitive) or Jesus' own faith (subjective genitive)? We are not sure of the answer, but we do have some clues to help us decide. One such clue is the reaction of the Judaizing missionaries who came after Paul to the churches in Galatia. They are appalled at Paul's theology. It was scandalous and they took it upon themselves to bring a correction to Paul. The Judaizers emphasized following the law and doing good works precisely because they were so uncomfortable with the unconditionality of Paul's grace-oriented theology. Certainly, we must to "do" something to be justified before God, to re-enter the righteous life! Paul would say emphatically, "No! We do nothing, Jesus does everything." We enter the kingdom of God, the community of compassion, our salvation, without doing anything. We simply allow ourselves to be loved and it is that love which changes us. It is like the unconditional love of a parent for a rebellious child. The parent continually offers only love and it is that love which sometimes brings a funda-mental change to the rebellion. You may know of an example where a parent loves a child into goodness. Of course, there are other examples of someone who continually rejects such love, but that child will never earn the parent's love by his or her good behavior. The parent's love always comes first and is not conditioned on the behavior of the child. God's love is like that and that is why the preferred translation of the preposition in Paul's letter to the Galatians chapter 2, verses 16 and 17, is subjective genitive. It is the faith and love of Jesus which saves us.

If, indeed, the "faith in Jesus" is the "faith of Jesus," we assume Jesus as faith toward God. Faith for Jesus is not the assurance that God merely exists, faith is a deep trust in the goodness and grace of God even in the face of tragedy, trauma, and injustice. There is a divine goodness, beauty in creation despite much evidence to the contrary; for Jesus to have faith means he trusts this divine goodness even while being nailed to the cross. Jesus shows us faith as trust not faith as a belief system and such faith is what Paul tries to teach the Galatians. Jesus' faith then is also toward us in the sense that Jesus loves us and has faith that we can live into the life God intends. Another way of putting it is that Jesus puts us in right relationship with God and the universe and we simply live into that relationship. We become the justified, good people Jesus sees in us, but it is Jesus' vision of us that comes first not our good works. The Judaizers always wanted our good works to come before our justification and then, of course, we would be the ones doing the salvation, not Jesus.

James, the brother of Jesus, was someone who would have interpreted the phrase, "faith in Jesus" as our faith toward Jesus. James would further state that our faith is to be lived out in good works. "You see that a person is justified by works and not by faith alone" (Jas 2:23). James also writes, ". . . so faith without works is also dead" (Jas 2:26). It appears James directly contradicts Paul, but maybe the contradiction can become a blessing. Taking Paul's emphasis on justification by the faith of Jesus only at a surface level, believers might be tempted to conclude that we don't need to do any works at all. We are saved by what Jesus has done and nothing we do, so let's not do anything. James's emphasis on works and faith going together might find some agreement with Paul if we consider works as our response to Jesus' faith.

In Galatians 5:22, 23, Paul describes good works as the "fruits of the spirit" and lists the following virtues: "love, joy, peace, patience, kindness, generosity, faithfulness, gentleness, and self-control." This wonderful list of virtues looks significantly like "works," but Paul is very careful with the metaphor used here. "Fruits" are an outgrowth, the product, of a healthy tree. For people to bear good fruit the inner soul should be healthy, therefore Paul's concern is about who we are—our core being. It is the faith of Jesus which affirms, redeems, justifies our core being and it is the fruits or works which follow. James is not so careful with his description of works and it is easy to be left with the impression that good works are required of us to earn justification. James may or may not have intended such an impression, but we can be left with the idea that if we are not doing good works, we should simply try harder. This impression ultimately leads to both faith and our ethical behavior as fully our own accomplishments. We, then, can become arrogant, complacent, or frozen in guilt, depending upon our successes and failures. Paul is careful to free us from this works righteousness spiral by taking the emphasis off ourselves. It is God who creates us good and God who, in Jesus, redeems us from evil and brokenness. Paul here can be a correction to a reading of James which overemphasizes good works, and James can be a corrective to those who interpret Paul and "faith alone" as license to do anything. Paul and James may be closer to agreement than it appears at first reading; both would agree that it is God who gets all the credit for our justification and we who respond with faith and good works—fruits of the spirit.

Discussion Questions

1. Paul says we are "justified by faith, not works." James says, "faith without works is dead." They directly contradict each other. Can each have value? How?

2. "Justified by grace through faith" is the central theme of Lutheran theology. We are saved by what God does, not by what we do. We are saved to go to heaven after we die but there is also a sense that "salvation" means we are made whole and healthy now. Describe your own character, priorities, and ethics if you were fully living the gift of salvation in the present. Because God is also concerned about the human community, what would a "salvation" society look like?

3. When James speaks of "works," it is similar to Paul's description of the "fruits of the spirit"—love, joy, peace, patience, kindness, gentleness, etc. Fruits grow naturally and do not have to be coerced. Maybe James and Paul can find some common ground when our ethics are motivated and inspired by God's loving relationship with us. Please describe one of your own loving relationships which have motivated your actions in a positive way.

4. Our good works don't effect salvation, they reflect salvation. We are not bad people who must work hard to be worthy, instead we are made good and holy by God and so we naturally begin producing the fruits of the spirit when we live out our relationship with God. Please react to that statement.

5. Consider effective parenting. Which is the better motivation: (1) parents who see their children as incapable

and in need of correction or (2) parents who see their children as competent and in need of guidance? How is this related to the grace/works debate?

Chapter Eight

End of the World: Exclusive vs. Inclusive

Eschatology is a theological word which means the study of the "last things" or the "end times." It assumes history is not cyclical as in some religious traditions, but linear and proceeding toward some culmination. That culmination is usually interpreted in the Christian tradition as a time of judgment when some are condemned, and others are saved to go to heaven. The Bible has many passages which lend themselves to this exclusive interpretation; also, Christian eschatology has been heavily influenced by post-biblical literature and theology. Judgment, separation, and a traumatic end of world have dominated much of Christian preaching and teaching throughout history. Literature has also picked up the theme of judgment, e.g., Dante's poetic masterwork *Inferno* vividly describes both the descent into the punishment of hell and the ascent to the glories of the many levels of heaven. In recent years the best-selling book series *Left Behind* assumes an end time culmination which separates the lost from the saved. Such exclusive interpretations rely on selected biblical passages which may be familiar to the reader.

We have read in passages such as Matthew 25:31 that the end times will include separation of the lost from the saved. Mark 13:8 says that great trauma will be associated with the end times: "Nation will rise against nation, and kingdom against kingdom; there will be earthquakes in various places; there will be famine. This is but the beginning of the birth pangs." Luke has a major section on the end times in his chapter 21, and Paul writes about the culmination of time in 1 Thessalonians and 1 Corinthians. The book of Daniel, in the Old Testament, describes the end times using what is called "apocalyptic" literature. The word "apocalypse" is a Greek word that means a "revealing or an uncovering." Today "apocalypse" has come to signify some great and traumatic end of existence catastrophe, which is not the strict meaning of the word. Revelation or apocalypse was not about predicting the future; rather it was getting to the core of things. Apocalyptic literature does so by using strange symbols and images which some compare to our dreams. When we dream, the images often make little sense, but modern psychology has taught us that dreams uncover our deepest feelings, fears, and hopes. We have unconscious concerns buried deep in our psyches and dreams are ways for those concerns to rise to the surface. Where our individual dreams unveil our personal core, apocalypse reveals our collective unconscious. Reading apocalyptic literature will show us there is great trauma and fear at society's core but, especially at the end of the book of Revelation, there is also a divine vision of goodness, peace, harmony, and joy.

The primary work of apocalyptic literature in the New Testament is the book of Revelation, the last book in the Bible. Revelation has usually been interpreted/experienced as an example of exclusive eschatology, where lost and saved are separated, but as we will see, the book also has some important images which support an inclusive eschatology where all creation is brought to a positive culmination and there is no need to emphasize who is lost and who is saved.

The book of Revelation, or the "Apocalypse," was written in the first century by someone named John on the Isle of Patmos off the coast of present-day Turkey. We do not know if this John was the disciple John or some other writer who simply used a famous name as a pseudonym, a practice which was common in the first century. We do know that the author wrote in the context of the Roman Empire's increasing tension with the rising Christian movement as there are many symbolic references to the tyranny of Rome. As we summarize parts of Revelation, we do so with thanks to two wonderful and in-depth studies of the book. These works are available to scholars and lay people and will help the student appreciate the full sweep of Revelation's meaning. One, is a lecture series by the Great Courses (see thegreatcourses. com) titled "Apocalypse: Controversies and Meaning in Western History" featuring Dr. Craig Koester of Luther Seminary, Saint Paul, Minnesota.[1] The second is a book written by Lutheran School of Theology, Chicago, professor Dr. Barbara Rossing. The book *The Rapture Exposed: The Message of Hope in the Book of Revelation* is published by Basic Books in 2005 and available in book stores, including Amazon. Many of their wise insights will be shared here.

Interpreting the book of Revelation can take many directions. The most familiar interpretation is Revelation as a road map to predict future events. The *Left Behind* series is one example of Revelation being interpreted as a prediction

1. See also Koester, *Revelation and the End of Things*.

of an exclusive end of the world. Interestingly, the interpretation which inspired the Left Behind series is quite recent, developed by a man named John Nelson Darby, whose dates are 1800–1882. Darby is the one who popularized the doctrine of the end times rapture, merging it with dispensationalism, the tribulation, and millennialism. There are many options to study these eschatological doctrines (e.g., Koester and Rossing), and we will here only give brief definitions. Dispensationalism is the idea that time is divided into certain "dispensations" as God works in history. One of the final "dispensations" is the thousand-year reign of Christ on earth, which is called the "millennium." There are two kinds of millennialisms, one is premillennialism, which teaches that Jesus will return and rule the earth for a thousand years before the world ends; and the second is postmillennialism, which says there will be a thousand-year reign of peace and then Jesus returns to usher in the world's end. Prior to, or after, the millennium will be a great "tribulation" of earthly suffering which all good Christians will avoid by being suddenly "raptured" or brought up to heaven. This dominant and somewhat convoluted analysis of Revelation, introduced and popularized by Darby beginning in 1830, is only one way to look at Revelation, and other interpretations are more convincing.

More recent scholars, such as Koester, Rossing, and Marcus Borg,[2] have emphasized Revelation as a document written in the context of the dominant political organization at the time—the Roman Empire. Rome and its empire are the "beast" and the "prostitute" described in Revelation and these scholars emphasize the social/political nature of

2. See Koester, *Revelation and the End of Things*, 30–31.

John's writing. The "empire" of Jesus would be based on a different set of values than that of Rome—justice, compassion, and peace, as opposed to violence, coercion, and economic power. This more sociopolitical interpretation is an alternative to the Darby interpretation and probably more accurate to the actual intent of the author John and very much worth the reader's further study. The point we are trying to make in this book, however, is about contradiction; and Revelation has within it the contradiction of exclusive and inclusive eschatology.

Exclusive eschatology, like that developed by Darby and many others, emphasizes the separation of people into two groups—the lost and the saved—and typically those people who hold such views consider themselves part of the saved group. The danger in such interpretation is obvious as it plays into our human tendency to tribalism where there is an "us versus them" divide. Exclusive eschatology mixed with human tribal tendencies has caused no end of suffering, prejudice, hatred, and even ethnic cleansing. The frightening imagery and symbolism in Revelation also touch a part of our own core unconscious, and our collective unconscious, which is fearful, anxious, competitive, and devious. Our nightmares reveal this shadowy side of our human nature, and it is our collective shadow side which can elect a politician like Hitler, demonize minorities, and glorify one's own "tribe." Exclusive eschatology, and especially Revelation, address this shadow side, this sinfulness, by providing us an escape route. We can flee all the danger and threat and find comfort with the other saved people in a glorious heaven, or some ideal earthly enclave of separated believers. Historically, Christianity has interpreted the Bible in ways which have led directly to Darby's kind of rapture theology where a few are saved but many are condemned. There is, however, a thread of eschatology that is more inclusive than the dominant exclusive strain and the sociopolitical comes close to celebrating this alternative.

The Bible itself contradicts the exclusive eschatology of people like John Nelson Darby and we find one example in the final vision of Revelation itself. In Revelation chapter 21, John has a vision of the end times. It is a dream in which he sees a city—a New Jerusalem—coming down out of heaven and he hears a voice. "See, the home of God is among people: he will dwell with them as their God; they will be his peoples, and God himself will be with them; he will wipe away every tear from their eyes. Death will be no more; mourning and crying and pain will be no more, for the first things have passed away" (Rev 21:3, 4). We notice the inclusive nature of the vision. It is the holy city that comes down to us. The word "peoples" is used to emphasize all the human communities not just a chosen one. The city is further described by John and it is also inclusive. There will be twelve gates to this new holy city and the gates will "never be shut by day and there will be no night there" (Rev 21:25). In Revelation 21:16, the city is described: "The city lies foursquare, its length the same as its width; and he measured the city with his rod, fifteen hundred miles; its length and width and height are equal." The city of God is a 1,500-mile cube! That is a big city, enough space for all the people of history to dwell! There is no temple in the city for God will dwell in every part of the city and the glory of the Lord God will be its light (Rev 21:23) and "the nations will walk by its light" (Rev 21:24). The inclusive eschatology continues with the imagery of light and a reference to the "nations," literally in Greek the word is "ethnic groups." Again, the city is not limited to a chosen group but all the ethnic groups.

Of course, John's vision of the holy city is not a literal description of the end times, but it is such a positive, joyful, and inclusive image that it counters the shadowy and frightening imagery found earlier in Revelation. This overwhelmingly optimistic culmination of history seems to include all people and all creation, and it is through this optimistic lens that we can view passages that appeal to the exclusive eschatology. For example, embedded within John's vision of the holy city is the following verse: "But as for the cowardly, the faithless, the polluted, the murderers, the fornicators, the sorcerers, the idolaters, and all liars, their place will be in the lake of fire and sulfur, which is the second death" (Rev 21:8). A verse like this can be used by exclusive theology to bolster its claims of separation, condemnation and punishment for the many and salvation for the selected group or chosen few. Reading the verse in the context of the rest of the holy city vision and realizing that all of us are named in the list of sinners—remember it says "all liars"—we must conclude that the "lake of fire" is some kind of refining fire which purges us of our sin and shadow side—the side that comes out in our nightmares. Would it not be wonderful to purged of our fear, insecurity, anger and prejudice? In Revelation 21:27 another verse can be viewed with optimistic inclusive eschatology eyeglasses, "But nothing unclean will enter it [Holy City], nor anyone who practices abomination or falsehood, but only those written in the Lamb's book of life." Again, the preceding verse seems to contradict the inclusive eschatology of a Holy City for all peoples. When we look at this verse with our optimistic lens, we realize that when it says "nothing unclean will enter" we are all excluded because none of us are "clean," that is, except for the grace God offers through Christ. Maybe it is the case that we are all written into the Lamb's Book of Life, for it is indeed true that none of us deserves entry into the New Jerusalem, and if Christ died to save us, could he not save all of us? Indeed, would he not save all of us? Imagine the result if our theology taught us that all people are written in the Lamb's Book of Life! We would not emphasize a line of separation between lost and saved, but a circle of inclusion which is big enough for all to join. If all people were written in the Lamb's Book of Life we would no longer consider anyone the "other."

Applying the biblical contradiction—exclusive versus inclusive eschatology—to our discussion of our unconscious, both personal and collective, we are left with a decision to make. An emphasis on exclusive eschatology and its divisive imagery appeals to what Carl Jung would call our shadow side.[3] Our tendency to fear and despise those different from ourselves—the other—and results in a tribalism of "us versus them." Theologically, it is expressed as lost versus saved. "We" are saved and going to heaven and "they" are lost and condemned to hell.

An inclusive eschatology appeals to our highest nature, our optimism and our joy, and it seems to match the kind of world Jesus was creating in his ministry—a world where even the least are included. When we have our dreams, they are not just nightmares laying bare our innermost anxiety, they are also revelations of our hope. Martin Luther King Jr.'s most famous speech was "I Have a Dream." The biblical contradiction in eschatology speaks to both parts of our

---

3. See Academy of Ideas, "Carl Jung and the Shadow: The Hidden Power of Our Dark Side," https://academyofideas.com/2015/12/carl-jung-and-the-shadow-the-hidden-power-of-our-dark-side/.

unconscious and we, therefore, choose which vision is to dominate our worldview. We can legitimately argue for an exclusive eschatology, as Darby did, or we can embrace the inclusive eschatology of Revelation chapter 21.

An inclusive eschatology seems preferable as it matches the sweep of the biblical narrative which emphasizes God grace, forgiveness, and striving to return creation to the original vision of a "garden of Eden" world. God's intention was never for only a chosen few to be saved but for all. When God called Abraham and Sarah, God did so in order that all the world would be blessed (Gen 12:3). When God chose Israel as God's special people, it was not because they were somehow morally superior, rather they were small and ordinary; they would become a model community of how the whole world should live together (Deut 7:7). Isaiah 11:6 shares a vision of a good and peaceful world where "the wolf shall live with the lamb, the leopard shall lie down with the kid, the calf and the lion and the fatling together and a little child shall lead them." It is a vision using a different metaphor but the content is identical to John's vision of the holy city. Jesus' ministry of inclusion of those considered sinners and outsiders resonates with an inclusive eschatology. The book of Ephesians reads, "He has made known to us the mystery of his will, according to his good pleasure that he set forth in Christ, as a plan for the fullness of time, to gather up all things in him, things in heaven and things on earth" (Eph 1:9). This verse describes "all things" being gathered up into God, which expands salvation beyond humanity and to the created order itself.

When we allow an inclusive eschatology to orient our worldview, we are freed from the need to determine who is lost and who is saved. Instead, we are open to God's "garden of Eden" intention for all people and all creation. We see the "other" as God would, and we release our prejudices and our fear of those different from ourselves. On the other hand, we do not totally reject the gifts exclusive eschatology can bring. Exclusive eschatology takes evil seriously and casts it into a "lake of fire." There is great and despicable evil in this world and exclusive eschatology condemns it, burns it away. That evil which is condemned at the culmination of the world is within each of us. Some have controlled it more than others but none of us are truly good. Exclusive eschatology burns the evil—the chaff—within us with a purging love as intense as fire. All of us are then condemned and all of us are saved.

Discussion Questions

1. Please share your own experience with exclusive eschatology. For example, what movies, books, sermons, discussions, Bible verses, etc., have been instrumental in shaping your understanding of God's end of the world scenario?

2. What are some negative aspects of an exclusive eschatology?

3. What are your initial thoughts after reading about the possibility of an inclusive eschatology also present in Scripture?

4. Discuss the political ramifications of the apocalyptic imagery in Revelation, especially as they refer to the Roman Empire. Discuss the empires in our century or recent history and how Revelation might be a confrontation to powers of domination.

5. Read Isaiah 11:6–9 and discuss this vision. Try rewriting it using modern images.

Epilogue

Reflections

THIS BOOK *BLESSED CONTRADICTIONS* was inspired by years of biblical study with members of Holy Spirit Lutheran Church in Kirkland, Washington. Approaching the Bible as a sweeping narrative has helped our congregation understand what Martin Luther meant when he said the "gospel" must critique the Bible.[1] The Bible is filled with contradictions, and not just the theological differences between authors as highlighted in this book. There are individual passages which can be used either for or against almost any social, political, or moral issue we confront today. Usually, we already have an opinion regarding whatever the issue and we look for biblical passages supporting our predetermined views. Reading the Bible as sweeping narrative has allowed students over the years to discern the "gospel" or "good news" of the human-divine interaction and to find a thread of consistency which finds its way between the contradictions. It is this "thread," this gospel, which critiques the extremes of the contradictions.

The content of the "thread" of consistency in the Bible might be surprising to many readers, especially those heavily

1. See Luther, *Martin Luther's Basic Theological Writings*, 51.

influenced by reading only short, selected Bible passages. An important first insight gleaned from the narrative approach to biblical study is what appears to be how God changes. Especially in the Old Testament, we have God described as angry, repentant, transcendent, immanent, demanding, loving, etc. Although God's nature seems inconsistent, what we find by our narrative approach is that God is in relationship with us and the creation. We have been so heavily influenced by philosophical definitions of God, like omniscience (all-knowing), omnipresence (everywhere present), and omnipotent (all-powerful), that we equate God with some first principle that is always and forever perfectly consistent and usually remote. The authors of the Bible did not use philosophical categories to describe God, they used the metaphor of a living, growing, changing relationship. What is consistent about the Bible's portrayal of God is that God continually desires good for human beings and the entire creation. It is like loving relationship between spouses, or that between a parent and child. There are ups and downs but also a relational commitment which consistently desires good. God is always wooing, cajoling, yearning for humans to return to health, wholeness, and the comfort of a close relationship with the divine.

God in relationship with humanity is not the only insight which helps us understand the thread of consistent good news evident in the Bible. A surprising discovery for many of us as we read the Bible was the definite lack of emphasis on personal salvation. God seemed always to be more interested in creating a holy human community on earth. Moses shared the Ten Commandments as a way for human society to live justly. The prophets continually called the nation, not just individuals, back to justice and a right relationship with God. Jesus called a group of people to be disciples and he welcomed the rejected to form a new godly community which the gospel writer Matthew described as the kingdom of heaven. The Apostle Paul did not simply seek personal conversions, he established church communities throughout the eastern Mediterranean basin. Our American emphasis on personal salvation may be more influenced by our cultural celebration of individualism rather than our thorough study of Scripture. We often ask questions like, "Are you saved?" Or, "Do you know Jesus as your personal savior?" Taking the Bible's obvious focus on establishing a just society on earth, we might ask, "Are you connected to a healthy community?" Or, "How are you working to create, a 'garden of Eden' world?" Or, "Are you following Jesus' path of welcoming the stranger?" The overemphasis on personally going to heaven after we die is only a part of the biblical thread of good news. Living and following Christ in the present is also a major, if not the primary, goal of Scripture.

Another component of the thread of good news present in Scripture is inclusivity. Those who are left out are noticed by the biblical story and every effort is made to include them. In fact, not only are excluded people included in God's community, they are essential. God works to change the world and create a loving and just society through ordinary, lost, downtrodden and forgotten people. Consider Abraham and Sarah, Joseph, Moses, the prophets, teenaged Mary, Jesus' disciples, the Apostle Paul. They were all ordinary people through whom God was at work to change the world. God works from the bottom up in Scripture, not the top down; hence we continue to see God present in people like Mother Teresa, Gandhi, or that Sunday School teacher who so influenced your faith life. Knowing that God is present and working through the outsider, our theology of evangelism begins to change.

Traditionally, evangelism, which stems from the Greek word meaning "good new" or "gospel," has been thought of as converting those who are lost to become those who are saved. You "evangelize" someone by getting them to adhere to a certain set of doctrines about Jesus. After reading the biblical narrative and noticing the thread of God's good news and God's inclusivity, we understand "evangelism" to literally do "good news" to those around us. We are to do what God does—love, serve, and include those who are left out. Evangelism further means that we not only share how God has touched us, we look for the ways God is working through people we Christians have described as "lost." God can be sending us a message—a "good news"—from someone sleeping on the streets or who worships God differently than we do or who claims no religion whatsoever. Taking the biblical narrative seriously, we let go of the notion that "we have it and they don't." God is bigger than our theology or our church denominations or a set of doctrines. Reading the biblical narrative in totality shows us that God is loose in the world and present in the most unlikely places and people.

The insight of God's inclusivity became apparent to Holy Spirit Lutheran students years ago and has deeply influence our church's policies. Initially, we associated LGBTQ people with inclusivity and in 1998 we became a Reconciling in Christ congregation which in other denominations is often called "open and affirming." The inclusivity thread of good news, however, also manifested itself as we worked to include people with physical or mental disabilities. We learned

through our efforts of inclusion that we had something ι
learn from people who have been marginalized. God was at
work touching us through them.

Our reading of the entire biblical narrative also taught us
that the Bible is not about science, or even literal history,
although much of the Bible is historically factual. The Bible's
most important gift to us is its mythology. It is too bad the
word "myth" has come to mean something that is not true,
because "myth" properly understood, is not about facts, and
certainly not about science. A myth is a fundamental worldview which orients the existence of an individual, a clan,
or a nation. For example, the ancient Greeks told stories
about the war with Troy. Achilles, Agamemnon, Ajax, Od-
ysseus, and others were the warriors whose courage, skill,
and smarts earned them victory and fame. Was it all literally true? Maybe. The ruins of ancient Troy have been found
and evidence of warfare was present, but did the Trojan
War go according to the poetry of Homer in the Iliad and
the Odyssey? Probably not. Homer told his stories of the
Greek heroes to inspire the mythology of Greek society. The
"myth" of the Trojan War showed the values that formed
the foundation of the Greek world: courage, strength, com-
petition, honor, glory, wisdom, and perpetual warfare. The
ancient Egyptians told myths which celebrated the stability
and consistency of their millennia-old civilization. The na-
tive Americans told stories of human-creation harmony and
interdependence. Science itself, as taught in our schools, has
become a kind of mythology to understand our existence
as primarily materialistic. Recently, powerful myths have
come to us through the media—our movies and television
series often portray an individual or small group fighting

some powerful and corrupt organization, entity, or individual. The overmatched heroes or heroines use strength, skill, courage, and brains to outwit and outfight the oppressors. Such is the mythology which orients our society, inspires competitiveness, and affects our politics. There is evil out there, or over there, or in "those people," and we must resist it and use our abilities to defeat it/them.

Mythologies are the most important aspects of a society's identity. They are who we are and how we orient ourselves and our society in the world. The most important aspects of the Bible then are not historical facts, doctrines, or scientific explanations, but mythology. The Bible presents a way for us to orient ourselves in the world—a mythology which is more important than facts, doctrine, or science. The biblical myth includes an understanding of the created universe as more than mere material, as in the science mythology. The created order is dynamic not static, relational not isolated, and there is a divine presence we call God which permeates it and is moving creation toward a positive culmination. The Bible mythology says there is progress and a yearning for goodness as the universe unfolds. The Bible mythology celebrated compassion for the downtrodden, simplicity, respect for the creation, self-sacrifice and service, justice, equality, inclusivity, cooperation, devotion, and community. Imagine a biblical mythology orienting our society! Imagine the type of movies we would see! A biblical mythology presents values almost opposite to the aggressive and competitive values of the Greek and Roman world, and quite different as well from the modern American myths of individualism, materialism, and exceptionalism. Our interpretation of Scripture has often been more informed by our cultural myths which we read back into the biblical narrative. Reading the Bible as a long narrative can provide us a better thread, a gospel thread, by which we can allow Scripture and the values it extols to critique our society and our fundamental American mythology.

There are many biblical themes which comprise the thread of gospel consistency which help us critique the contradictions evident in Scripture and we have mentioned only a few of them here: God seems to change in Scripture only because the Bible describes God in a living, dynamic, but always loving, relationship with humanity and the creation; the Bible always seeks to include the excluded; the Bible, as a fundamental set of values for society, is a profound mythology more important than scientific fact. There are many other strands to the thread of the gospel running through Scripture—God's consistent grace and forgiveness, God working from the bottom of society up, a desire of justice and equality, God's care for the nonhuman parts of creation, and many more. There is one last strand we will mention here and that is the theology of the cross.

The Gospel of Mark most fully articulates an understanding of God who joins humans in the ups and downs of existence. God desires health, wholeness, goodness, and grace for all people and for the created order itself and seeks to achieve that goal, not by a remote top-down fiat, but rather by entering the human story and experiencing the pain and evil which afflict God's "garden of Eden" world. It is as if God on the cross absorbs that pain and evil, freeing humanity to live into the joy, peace, and justice God always intended. We get glimpses of that intention, that kingdom now, and we have faith God is pulling all things to a positive and complete culmination.

The theology of the cross fundamentally means God goes with us and experiences what we do. Jesus, of course, is the primary example of God entering our human story, but the thread exists throughout the Bible. In the garden of Eden God walked and talked with the humans. God is present with the Hebrew people as they wandered in the wilderness for forty years. God symbolically dwelled with the people in the holy of holies of the Jerusalem temple. God was like the suffering servant in the prophet Isaiah, and God was a still, small voice to Elijah in 1 Kings 19:12. A theology of the cross is an important, maybe the most important, strand in the thread of the gospel which Luther said must critique the Bible itself. It also critiques and guides our own life journeys and is central to our earthly purpose as individuals and as community.

A theology of the cross often becomes the core function of anyone who takes on the calling to be a pastor. It not only helps critique the extremes of biblical contradictions, it guides life and calling. A pastor carries many responsibilities: preacher, teacher, counselor, administrator, manager, visionary, organizer, motivator, comforter, etc. Years of ministry will show the pastor that the most important role is to live out the theology of the cross. All people, at one time or another, will go into some deep and difficult valley of despair—grief, loneliness, illness, fear, anxiety, anger, pain, etc. A pastor is often allowed into the valleys of these shadows, to walk with people in their most difficult moments. It is the greatest privilege a pastor knows. The pastor, in such situations, is not really him- or herself, but rather a symbol of what God does. The pastor is a stand-in—someone who represents the gospel, the good news of God's love, compassion, commitment, and presence in every human life.

The pastor, however, is not the only one who goes into the valleys with others. You, the reader, do so as well, and it may be the most important calling you have in life. Martin Luther was committed to something he called the "priesthood of all believers" which teaches us that we all mediate God's great and good love. Going with others into the pain of life does more than simply bring comfort, there is something salvific about it. The word "salvation" in the Bible means health, wholeness, and peace. Going with others into the deep valleys often can bring a holy sense of health, wholeness, and peace . . . even in hospice. It is as if no despair, and not even death, can dim the light of someone who cares. The light of compassion and love shared in that hospice room is the core of the gospel thread woven through the Bible and woven through our earthly life. God is the light of compassion, the light of salvation. God is Good Friday with us, and we are Easter Sunday with God.

Bibliography

Althaus, Paul. *The Theology of Martin Luther*. Translated by Robert C. Schultz. Philadelphia: Fortress, 1989.

Armstrong, Karen. *The Battle for God*. New York: Knopf, 2000.

———. *The Bible: A Bibliography*. New York: Grove, 2007.

———. *The Great Transformation: The Beginning of Our Religious Traditions*. New York: Anchor, 2007.

———. *A History of God: The 4000-Year Quest of Judaism, Christianity and Islam*. New York: Ballantine, 1993.

Aulen, Gustaf. *Chistus Victor: An Historical Study of the Three Main Types of the Idea of Atonement*. Translated by A. G. Herbert. American ed. New York: Macmillan, 1966.

Borg, Marcus J. *Jesus, a New Vision: Spirit, Culture, and the Life of Discipleship*. London: HarperSanFrancisco, 1993.

———. *Meeting Jesus Again for the First Time: The Historical Jesus & the Heart of Contemporary Faith*. San Francisco: HarperSanFrancisco, 1994.

Borg, Marcus J., and John Dominic Crossan. *The First Paul: Reclaiming the Radical Visionary behind the Church's Conservative Icon*. New York: HarperOne, 2009.

Brueggemann, Walter. *Genesis*. Interpretation. Atlanta: John Knox, 1982.

Forde, Gerhard O. *Where God Meets Man: Luther's Down-to-Earth Approach to the Gospel*. Minneapolis: Augsburg, 1972.

Grane, Leif. *The Augsburg Confession: A Commentary*. Translated by John H. Rasmussen. Minneapolis: Augsburg, 1987.

Heschel, Abraham J. *The Prophets*. Vol. 1. New York: Harper Colophon, 1969.

———. *The Prophets*. Vol. 2. New York: Harper Colophon, 1975.

Hicks, John, ed. *The Myth of Christian Uniqueness: Toward a Pluralistic Theology of Religions*. Maryknoll: Orbis, 1987.

Johnson, Luke Timothy. *Religious Experience in Earliest Christianity: A Missing Dimension in New Testament Studies*. Minneapolis: Fortress, 1998.

Kingsbury, J. D. *The Parables of Jesus in Matthew 13: A Study in Redaction-Criticism*. London: SPCK, 1969.

Koester, Craig R. *Revelation and the End of All Things*. Grand Rapids: Eerdmans, 2001.

Luther, Martin. *Lectures on the Psalms I (1–75)*. Edited by Hilton C. Oswald. Translated by Herbert J. A. Bouman. Luther's Works 10. Philadelphia: Fortress, 1957.

———. *Martin Luther's Basic Theological Writings*. Edited by Timothy F. Lull. Minneapolis: Fortress, 1989.

Malysz, Piotr. "Exegesis the Lutheran Way." *Lutheran Theology: An Online Journal*, December 17, 2013. https://lutherantheology.wordpress.com /2013/12/17/exegesis-the-lutheran-way/.

Miles, Jack. *God: A Biography*. New York: Knopf, 1995.

Nelson-Pallmeyer, Jack. *Jesus Against Christianity: Reclaiming the Missing Jesus*. Harrisburg, PA: Trinity International, 2001.

Pagels, Elaine H. *Revelations: Visions, Prophecy, and Politics in the Book of Revelation*. New York: Penguin, 2012.

Rossing, Barbara R. *The Rapture Exposed: The Message of Hope in the Book of Revelation*. Boulder, CO: Westview, 2005.

Schlink, Edmund. *Theology of the Lutheran Confessions*. Translated by Paul F. Koehneke and Herbert J. A. Bouman. Philadelphia: Fortress, 1967.

Wright, N. T. *Jesus and the Victory of God*. Vol. 2. Minneapolis: Fortress, 1996.